All Creatures

All
Creatures

LIFE LESSONS LEARNED
From Some of God's
Lesser Creatures

ELIZABETH SIMMONS

New York

All Creatures
Life Lessons Learned From Some of God's Lesser Creatures

Published in New York, New York, by Morgan James Publishing. Morgan James and The Entrepreneurial Publisher are trademarks of Morgan James, LLC.
www.MorganJamesPublishing.com

The Morgan James Speakers Group can bring authors to your live event. For more information or to book an event visit The Morgan James Speakers Group at www.TheMorganJamesSpeakersGroup.com.

Shelfie

A **free** eBook edition is available
with the purchase of this print book.

CLEARLY PRINT YOUR NAME ABOVE IN UPPER CASE

Instructions to claim your free eBook edition:
1. Download the Shelfie app for Android or iOS
2. Write your name in **UPPER CASE** above
3. Use the Shelfie app to submit a photo
4. Download your eBook to any device

ISBN 978-1-63047-846-9 paperback
ISBN 978-1-63047-848-3 eBook
ISBN 978-1-63047-847-6 hardcover
Library of Congress Control Number:
2015917345

Cover Design by:
Rachel Lopez
www.r2cdesign.com

Interior Design by:
Bonnie Bushman
bonnie@caboodlegraphics.com

In an effort to support local communities and raise awareness and funds, Morgan James Publishing donates a percentage of all book sales for the life of each book to Habitat for Humanity Peninsula and Greater Williamsburg

Get involved today, visit
www.MorganJamesBuilds.com

Habitat
for Humanity®
Peninsula and
Greater Williamsburg
Building Partner

Dedicated to my father, Richard Call,
who always encouraged me to use my gift of writing
to entertain people while also honoring God.
Though he is no longer physically here in this world,
he remains in my heart every moment of every day.
This is for you, Daddy.

Contents

Preface

If you know me at all, then you know that while there are many things that fill my life with untold pleasure, there is one thing in particular that really gets the warm fuzzies going inside of me: dogs. My dogs. Your dogs. Any dogs! I have fully prepared myself for the day that I am simply referred to as "the crazy dog lady." And I will not take offense should my future grandchildren decide to call me their "Woofy" or "BowWow."

My love for dogs has grown drastically since I became an adult—even more so since I became a mom. After all, owning a dog is similar in some ways to having children. They are both completely dependent on you for shelter, nourishment, discipline, love. But children have the advantage of spoken language. They can talk to you, and in the process of teaching your children, you can learn lessons from them as well. We know that dogs are more than capable of learning commands and tricks, but their lack of communication skills keeps them from being able to teach us anything in return. Or, does it?

Don't worry, I'm not going to tell you my dogs have learned to decipher the Greek alphabet and we have developed a method of communicating with each other using flashcards and a xylophone. What I am going to tell you is that I have learned a lot of valuable lessons from the parade of dogs that has marched through my life. (I've been taught a thing or two by a horse as well.)

I'm no theologian, and I've never studied philosophy or psychology. My background is very simple. I am the third of four daughters born to a Baptist preacher and his lovely bride in Fort Worth, Texas. Growing up, I was at church every time the doors were open: Sunday school, Sunday morning service, Sunday evening service and choir practice, Monday night prayer meeting, Tuesday night visitation, Wednesday evening service, and orchestra practice. You get the idea. As a result, God's infallible word and his unfailing promises have never been far from my heart.

As I have gotten older, it seems I am better able to recognize the promises of God in the ordinary, everyday events of life. And that is why I decided to write this book.

Those fantastic, four-legged friends of mine have reminded me on more than one occasion of lessons I learned in Sunday school all those years ago.

Chapter 1

God's Plans Aren't Always Our Plans

"For I know the plans I have for you," declares the Lord, "plans to prosper you and not to harm you, plans to give you hope and a future."
—Jeremiah 29:11

Mornings are always hectic when you have a teenage daughter. "Did you eat breakfast?" "Do you have your backpack?" "Did you grab your homework?" "We need to get going." "Do you need lunch money?" "Are you staying for biology tutorials this afternoon?" "We're going to be late!" It's always rush out the door, jump in the car, and hit the end of the driveway in seconds flat. Nothing can stop us now.

Did I say *nothing*? Let me take a moment here to say my youngest daughter, Sydney, shares my love of dogs. Actually, her love far surpasses mine because it encompasses just about *every* animal roaming the earth. So, of course, when we saw the pitiful little dog in the bar ditch across the street, we knew we would both be late that day. He seemed extremely timid, scared of anything and everything that crossed his path. We quickly devised a plan: we would see if we could successfully coax him into the car, then I would take him to work to try to find a home for him. (Fortunately for me, my office was filled with like-minded lovers of dogs.)

Sydney got out of the car and cautiously crossed the street, trying not to startle the poor guy too much. As she began her approach, he was planning his escape, slowly turning to trot away from her. She knew if she tried to pursue him, he might become more frightened and run into the street to face the morning traffic. So she aborted the mission and returned to the car. At least we tried.

The next evening, I was in the bedroom getting things ready for the following day when I heard my husband, Ken, calling to me from the kitchen. We met halfway between the two rooms, and in his arms, I saw a dirty lump of white fur, speckled with tiny brown dots. "Look what I found," was all he said as he turned to make his way to the back porch. It was the terrified dog Sydney and I had attempted to rescue the day before. Ken explained, "I was out closing up the barn and saw something crawling up to me real slow. As soon as he got close enough, he just rolled over at my feet and looked up at me as if to say, 'Just put me out of my misery.' Saddest thing I ever saw. Snuck up on me like a little ghost." I named him Casper, after the friendly ghost.

Turns out the tiny brown dots were fleas—hundreds of them. We found a number of ticks feeding on his undernourished body, several of them inside his ears. His pads were dry and cracked and looked like they would be painful to walk on. We put a soft blanket on the porch for him to sleep on, filled bowls with food and water, and gave him shelter for the night. The next morning we got him cleaned up, gave him a flea and tick treatment, and took him to the vet for vaccinations. We wanted to make sure he was in tip-top shape so we could try to re-home him; I was entrusted with this daunting task.

Now, because Ken knew when he married me what he was getting himself into, I believe he also knew when he carried that baby dog into our home that night, it would become a part of our family. So he couldn't have been surprised when I announced I had found a forever home for Casper—ours!

We didn't need another dog. At the time, we had three perfectly good dogs already. But what Casper didn't have— and desperately needed—was a perfectly good family. Here, one of the sweetest animals on the planet had been discarded like yesterday's trash. We don't know how he came to be alone on the streets, but he did. We don't know what caused him to approach Ken that night, but he did. We don't know why he chose our family, but he did. Of course, I have always seen it as divine intervention. Yes, I believe God planned for Casper to cross our path—in his perfect timing—so that he would be ensured a future with a loving family.

When we face uncertain times, we can hold on to the knowledge that God wants no harm to befall us. He has plans for us, plans to prosper us and give us hope and a future—even the very least of us.

Chapter 2

Storms of Life

Don't panic. I'm with you. There's no need to fear for I'm your God. I'll give you strength. I'll help you. I'll hold you steady, keep a firm grip on you.
—Isaiah 41:10 (MSG)

he sound of thunder rumbling in the night brought me to a place of semi-consciousness. Though I had not opened my eyes, I could clearly see the heaven-orchestrated laser light show through closed eyelids. Each thunder clap was accompanied by a tremor that shook the entire house. Ah, summer storms in Texas. And this was going to be a good one.

As parents of older children—five out on their own and only one teenager living at home—it's been years since severe thunderstorms have drawn a child to the sanctuary of our bedroom during the night. Surely this night would be no different. And yet, I had the sense something, or rather *someone*, was watching me.

Rolling over to face the bank of windows, I slowly opened my eyes. There beside the bed, backlit by the glow of continual lightning strikes, head barely visible above the height of the mattress, sat Bexar. Sweet baby Bexar, now four-and-a-half years old, is by far the most gentle, loving, loyal dog in all of creation. A mix of German shepherd and Labrador retriever, he was blessed with only the most endearing qualities of each breed—along with a healthy dose of storm anxiety. His fear of thunder and lightning doesn't cripple him; he doesn't destroy things or pace the floor or cry. He just wants to know that whatever happens, he will be surrounded by his family and that we will weather the storms together.

Those frightened, expectant eyes staring at me in the darkness of night reminded me so much of the days past when my children would come running in, seeking security. What choice did I have? I patted the bed and offered an invitation for him to join us. And just like those children, he quickly accepted, snuggling in between me and Ken as we stroked his fur and gave him the assurances he needed that everything was going to be all right.

We encounter many storms throughout life—and not just of the thunder and lightning variety. How about the shaky economy storm? Or the sketchy job market storm? Or my personal favorite, the raising teenagers storm? All these scenarios are just as frightening to this grown woman as a thunderstorm is to a small child (or dog). The storms of life are inevitable. But we never have to face them alone, and we certainly are not meant to fear. God tells us as plain as day, "Don't panic, I'm with you" (Isaiah 41:10 MSG).

Bexar's anxiety reminds me that I can always trust the promises God has made to me. If I do, as sure as Bexar finds comfort in the arms of his family, I will find comfort in the arms of God.

Chapter 3

Give Me Ears to Hear

The LORD said, "Go out and stand on the mountain in the presence of the LORD, for the LORD is about to pass by." Then a great and powerful wind tore the mountains apart and shattered the rocks before the LORD, but the LORD was not in the wind. After the wind there was an earthquake, but the LORD was not in the earthquake. After the earthquake came a fire, but the LORD was not in the fire. And after the fire came a gentle whisper.

—1 Kings 19:11–12

 am always amazed at the superior hearing our dogs have been gifted with. They can decipher the sound of Ken's truck when he comes

9

home in the evenings before I can even see it approaching. And there is no chance of the kids sneaking in past curfew because the dogs alert us long before they get a hand on the front door knob. I do notice, however, that sometimes their hearing seems to fail them. Take Bexar, for instance. He loves to be outside, lying in the cool grass, taking in the fresh air, chasing squirrels and grasshoppers. When it's time to come in, we go to the door and call him, but sometimes those super-keen ears don't seem to be working properly. He usually gets a couple of chances to make things right before we have to get down to business and grab the whistle. One long blast on the whistle and here he comes a-running. It seems like he may suffer from a condition many of us humans refer to as "selective hearing."

On the other hand, Dixie doesn't seem to be afflicted with a hearing deficiency. Generally speaking, you just have to get the "D" out, and she is at your side in a flash. But it's not just our voices that she responds to instantly. Contrary to some of the opinions within our home, Dixie is a very intelligent dog. She learns quickly and remembers assigned cues well. For instance, when I am shutting down the computer for the evening, as soon as she hears the beep signaling that Windows is closing, she gets up and stands at the door to wait for me. She associates that sound with my leaving the room.

Let me give you a little insight into the mind of Dixie Anne Simmons. First, she is *my* dog. No one else in the house will have her. She is a two-year-old Weimaraner and is true to her breed in every way: hyperactive, high strung, territorial, loyal to a fault, seemingly constructed of Velcro, the whole nine yards. She is also a canine vacuum when it comes to food. (I'm sure this is genetic since I, too, love to eat!) Here's where her supersonic hearing comes into play.

Let's assume we've enjoyed a fun-filled day of activity at the lake and have returned home with dogs that are completely worn out. They come in the house, quench their thirst, and hit the tile floor to crash for hours. Dixie curls up like a delicate little fawn on her bed by the bay window. She's out cold in seconds flat. How do we know this? Because she snores like a grizzly bear! An hour or so into her nap, my husband makes his way to the kitchen for a snack. He opens the pantry, rummages through the assortment of items up for grabs, selects a honey bun—or something of equal nutritional value—and opens the wrapper. In a flash, Dixie is wide awake, racing into the kitchen to convince her daddy to share his goodies with her. Mind you, she was in a coma just thirty seconds ago, and the kitchen pantry is a good ten yards from the dog bed. Yet she heard that faint rustling of paper and responded. Instantly. This is the sound Dixie longs to hear each and every day. It beckons her to come, and come she does because she associates the sound with something good.

Just like Dixie, I need to have ears to hear God calling me and the desire to respond to his call instantly. His still, small voice speaks to me daily, but if I don't listen for it, I will miss it. And in missing God's call, I also miss the "something good" that is associated with it.

Chapter 4

Excuse Me, but Isn't It Time to Eat?

There is a time for everything, and a season for every activity under the heavens.
—Ecclesiastes 3:1

Who among us doesn't love a well-organized schedule? You know, the kind that keeps you on task each and every day. Without fail, it reminds you to do exactly what needs to be done at the precise moment it is required. Some people keep track of their daily activities by consulting a traditional, notebook-style organizer, such as a Day-Timer or Day Runner. There are those who are more technologically advanced, preferring to utilize the calendar on their smart phone or enlisting the aid of one of any number of available apps. And still there are a few who would rather take a more personal approach to maintaining their appointments. These people pick up the phone and call their spouse. "Honey, was I supposed to pick Johnny up from basketball practice *today*?"

To each his own, I guess. Me? I use a DayWeimer. Because Dixie has such a precise internal clock, I can pretty much set my schedule around her. I don't even own a watch anymore. She is generally accurate to within five minutes in either direction. Here's how it works:

My day begins with her jumping onto the bed, as delicately as eighty-five pounds of Weimaraner can bound onto a bed. She eases over to rest her chin on my shoulder and looks at me with those eyes that say, "Excuse me, but isn't it time to eat breakfast?" I look over at the clock on the nightstand that reads six o'clock and confirm that it is, indeed, time to eat breakfast. So we get out of bed, eat our morning meal, and start knocking out items on our to-do list.

After loading up the list with several check marks (who among us doesn't love checking off things we've completed throughout the day?) and typically when I am in the middle of a project that requires a great deal of concentration, I feel a cold, wet nose nudging my elbow. It finally pushes my arm out of the way, allowing just enough clearance for a little Weimer chin to rest on my thigh. Again, those eyes: "Excuse me, but isn't it time to eat lunch?" Sure enough, the clock on the computer shows midday, high noon, lunch time. Obviously, we must stop what we're doing to enjoy the afternoon meal together so we can then return our focus to the list.

Eventually, it's time to clean up my mess and put away my toys for the day. And exactly how do I know when it's time to do this? My DayWeimer alerts me when it is five o'clock, on the dot. She uses what we refer to as the "Velcro dog" move to get my attention. She quietly sidles up to me and ever so slowly eases her weight against my legs. It's not enough pressure to knock me over, just enough to make me aware that there's a Weimaraner stuck to my leg. What do I see when I look down at her? You guessed it, her "Excuse me, but isn't it time to eat supper?" eyes. And because she's right, we do.

There are instances when her clock is running a little fast, and she tries to give the signal too early. In those cases, she gets an unfavorable response: "Not yet . . . just wait a little longer." She puts on her pouty face and dramatically plops into her chair or bed and proceeds to stare at me until it *is* time to eat again.

Every day we go through these motions, and every day it's as if I'm seeing my reflection in a mirror. All too often I catch myself nudging God's hand, nosing my way into his lap and saying, "Excuse me, but isn't it time for me to have this thing?" or "Isn't it time for you to give me that thing?" or "Isn't it time for this thing to happen?" Occasionally, we are in agreement, and the thing I ask of him is granted, but that is not always the case. More often than not, I get what I consider to be an unfavorable response: "Not yet . . . just wait a little longer." A lot of times, I take this news pretty hard. I may even whine about it for a while, sometimes for a very long while. But deep down inside, I know that God's timing is always perfect and that I will never miss out on a golden opportunity if I'm waiting on him.

While I may know in my head there is a time for everything, God alone knows when that appointed time is. And like Dixie, sometimes I have to be patient and "just wait a little longer."

Chapter 5

Whatcha Thinkin' About?

Finally, brothers and sisters, whatever is true, whatever is noble, whatever is right, whatever is pure, whatever is lovely, whatever is admirable—if anything is excellent or praiseworthy—think about such things.

—Philippians 4:8

From the day we brought Dixie into our home, we noticed that she had a constant, voracious appetite. She could clean a bowl in seconds flat. Seriously, our son timed her one day. She finished two heaping cups of dry kibble in seventeen seconds.

We knew we wanted her to get accustomed to being on the same feeding schedule as the other dogs, so we added her bowls to the lineup each morning and evening. Unfortunately, that didn't seem to work for her. We tried increasing the number of meals she received each day and decreasing the amount of food per meal. We assumed that by receiving the same amount of food, but with less waiting time between meals, she wouldn't feel famished all the time. Not so. It didn't seem to matter how much we fed her or how frequently it was offered, she just could not get full.

A new plan was in order. Enter Plan B; it was agreed that we would just feed her until she stopped eating. This would surely give us an estimate of how much food it would take to satisfy her hunger. Imagine mucking a barn—digging that shovel in and tossing your treasure into a wheel barrow. That's what it was like feeding Dixie. Scoop after scoop was transferred from food bin to bowl. I am convinced that if we hadn't stopped dishing out the grub, she would still be eating that meal today. She just wouldn't stop. She was a bottomless pit!

Obviously, Plan B was a complete and utter failure. We were going to have to pull out the big guns and summon the help of the keeper of all knowledge: Google. I hit the Internet and started researching dog food options. My husband believed if we upgraded to a higher-end food with agreater protein content, we would be able to curb Dixie's appetite. Armed with all the information we needed to make an informed food decision, we loaded up and headed in to the big city.

Thanks to a helpful manufacturer's representative present at the pet supply store, we walked out with thirty pounds of high-protein dog food and a wealth of information as to why this sweet baby girl could not get her belly full on the food we were previously feeding her. That evening, we carefully followed the manufacturer's directions for properly acclimating her to the new food. After only one feeding (which was half the size of her normal portion) she calmly retired to her bed and slept the night away. We had been depending on fillers and multiple byproducts to quell her appetite, but it always left her hungry for more. Once we began to feed her a high-protein food—something with a little more substance to it—she was able to satisfy her hunger and leave the bowl feeling full and content.

Dixie's dilemma isn't so different from one we face each day. It doesn't involve food for physical nourishment, but food for thought. As with the food we use to fuel our bodies, we are faced with many choices relating to what we will fuel our minds with each day. When we allow our minds to be fueled by ideas and images that lack substance, we may experience a mini high—a laugh or a spark of excitement—but it is only temporary. It will soon leave us with nothing but a hunger for something else. Many of us will spend months, even years, repeatedly frequenting the same shallow suppliers of momentary thrills but never finding satisfaction. For example, many of the Facebook pages I subscribe to are filled with little gems of wisdom and encouragement that I gladly welcome into my mind, but many of them are not.

We are reminded in Philippians 4:8 to fill our minds with things that are true, noble, right, pure, lovely, and admirable, to think about things that are excellent and praiseworthy. By closely monitoring our thought diet, we can be assured we will come away from every mind meal feeling full and completely satisfied, rather than feeling empty and hungry for something more.

If I only fuel my mind with ideas and images that are empty and devoid of substance, I will always leave the table feeling hungry, searching for alternate means of fulfillment. But if I increase the amount of true, noble, right, pure, lovely, and admirable things that are available to feed my mind, I can push my plate away, feeling full and wholly satisfied, like Dixie now does.

Chapter 6

The Waiting Is
the Hardest Part

*The Lord is good to those who wait for him, to the soul
who seeks him. It is good that one should wait quietly
for the salvation of the Lord.*
—Lamentations 3:25–26 (ESV)

Congratulations are in order in our home, as we have recently added a new member to the family. We are now the proud grandparents of a handsome black and white terrier mix, approximately three months old and weighing in at exactly twelve pounds. Our newest granddog's name is Tydis. He was rescued from a local animal shelter and has been given permanent sanctuary in our home. In the short time he has been with us, he has secured his place in the pack and has begun to fit in extremely well. As a matter of fact, he's asleep on my lap at this very moment. (And if I said I didn't absolutely love it, I would be telling a big, fat lie.)

Our youngest son, Brady, celebrated his fifteenth birthday a little over a week ago. For years, he has made countless requests for a puppy, and for years, each and every one of them has been denied. Now, don't get me wrong here. Ken and I are in full agreement that every boy should have a four-legged friend to grow up with. After all, what little guy doesn't want a dog of his very own for a running buddy, personal shadow, devoted pal, and bedtime snuggle bug? The idea of a young boy being followed around by his tiny, tail-wagging companion warms our hearts. And Brady is certainly no exception to this rule.

However, like most adolescent males currently inhabiting this planet, he has given us no indication that he is ready to care for another living creature day in and day out. If owning a dog requires an enormous commitment on Brady's part, taking on the responsibility of a puppy will be monumental. We know this because we have adopted both puppies and dogs in the past. It is our humble opinion that if you made a list of pros and cons comparing the two, the only thing puppies would add to the "pros" column is their cuteness, and they outgrow that rather quickly.

Another factor we had to take into account when shooting down this sweet, young man's dream was the number of dogs already making their home with us. At one point, we were sharing our humble 1,800 square foot abode with four dogs, and that got quite hairy at times—both figuratively and literally! As time passed and our older children moved out of the house to pursue the next chapter of their lives, we realized two things: (1) we were left with only two canine residents and (2) Brady had developed into a very responsible young man. He was nearing the end of his freshman year when we started putting together the ground rules for puppy ownership.

A few days later, with joyful hearts, we requested that Brady join us for what we refer to as a "family forum." Family forum originated as a means of getting everyone in the same room at the same time to give his or her opinion on important decisions that would ultimately affect the entire family. A great example is when Ken was presented with a job offer that would require him to travel quite a bit. Since his absence would mean the rest of us would have to take over his responsibilities while he was away, we needed the input of the affected family members. Over time, the content of family forum has changed somewhat, but its purpose has remained steadfast: to invite open discussion of any topic that has an effect on the family. The meeting can be called by anyone for any reason, and all resident family members are required to attend.

Our family forum for the puppy was small, just Ken, Brady, and me. We praised Brady for the strides he was making toward becoming a fine, upstanding, young man. We acknowledged the ways we had seen his level of responsibility grow in recent months. And then we told him he had earned the privilege of selecting a puppy of his own. After removing only a very small portion of the big-idiot grin from his face, he grabbed the laptop and began his online search for adoptable puppies.

In case you have forgotten, or you honestly don't know this, finding the perfect puppy takes a great deal of time and effort. It is not something to be entered into lightly. We're talking weeks, months even, of painstakingly searching rescue site after rescue site, researching breed after breed. Your lifelong furry soul mate doesn't just fall into your lap. Typically.

Last Saturday, Brady agreed to accompany me on one of my least favorite adventures—grocery shopping. And what better place to acquire the perfect puppy than the Wal-Mart parking lot? We passed a truck with what appeared to be bloodhound pups in the back and a freshly painted cardboard sign nearby that practically screamed: "Free Puppies!" I was not opposed to the idea, but I reminded Brady that we could not just show up at home with a puppy. He needed to confirm the acquisition with the CEO first, and he could do that while I grabbed groceries. By the time he got the all clear, I would be done, and we could pick his pup.

Unfortunately, the negotiations and the shopping took longer than expected, and needless to say, the truck was long gone by the time we made our way back to it. Oh, the disappointment in that boy's eyes! There was heartbreak clearly visible on his face, and that brought pain to this mamma's soul. We were only a couple of blocks from the local animal shelter and I didn't have too many perishables, so I suggested we swing by to see what they had available for adoption. And there he was.

Tydis, a handsome black and white terrier mix, approximately three months old and weighing in at exactly twelve pounds. There was no doubt this was Brady's perfect puppy. They were meant for one another. Ty had been patiently waiting for over a month to be rescued, and he recognized his savior as soon as the two made eye contact. Their patience had paid off, and their reward was great.

Ty's rescue, and Brady's reward, reminds me that the Lord is good to those who wait for him. Waiting on God, seeking his will over our own, can be difficult. And how much more difficult it is to wait *quietly*. When we want something, we want to scream, "NOW!" We fear, thinking, *If I don't get it now, it might be gone later, and then what?* We might actually receive the greater blessing God has already prepared for us. And isn't it that much sweeter to receive God's blessings in his time rather than our desires on demand?

Chapter 7

Walk by Faith

For we walk by faith, not by sight.
—2 Corinthians 5:7 (NKJV)

A few years ago, I heard a song by native Texas country artist Sunny Sweeney that touched me in the deepest part of my soul. It was filled with such genuine and insightful lyrics. I knew the first verse alone could be the theme song for how I felt about life. Let me share just a few lines with you: "If I could make my living going fishing, then I would make my living with a line and pole, put food on the table, pay the money to the landlord, buy some working clothes 'cause I ain't making money going fishing like I'm paid in a factory." It's pure poetry, I'm tellin' ya.

That's right, folks, I love to fish. As a matter of fact, our entire family enjoys fishing together. I recall being creekside with Ken one weekday, both our lines in the water and a couple of decent-sized crappie on the stringer. Our picture-perfect moment was interrupted by a ringing cell phone. Our daughter, Kimberly—then a senior in high school and dependent on us for transportation—called to say she had been released early and needed a ride home from school. Without divulging my current location, I asked if there was any way she could hitch a ride with someone. She said she had already tried and could find no one to help her out. I reluctantly left my husband in charge of our gear and drove to the school. When I explained that she had interrupted my outing and that's why I needed her to get a ride elsewhere, she was momentarily appalled. But she quickly recovered and said, "Well, let's make sandwiches and get back down there!" Now *that's* what I'm talking about!

Seriously, though, for me, one of the simplest pleasures in this life is getting up at dawn, heading down to the creek, and spending the morning with a line or two in the water. Sometimes we fish; other times we *catch* fish; and every now and then we just enjoy the peace and quiet that a hidden creek affords.

Occasionally, when the kids have made other plans, Ken and I will steal away for some evening bank fishing. On one of our getaways, we requested the company of royalty. Calamity Jane, an "overly healthy" black chow mix, enjoyed a position of tenure in the family and was affectionately referred to as "the Queen." Ken adopted her from a shelter when she was just over a year and a half. She had been injured in a car accident and was recuperating from hip surgery when he rescued her. He remembers walking in and being met by a host of healthy dogs, barking and jumping, vying for his attention, when his gaze fell on Calamity. Curled into a tight ball in the corner with her bum leg bandaged, she looked up at him with soulful eyes, and he said, "How 'bout that one?"

We also invited Calamity's dear friend, Mocha, to join us that evening. A sweet, middle-aged chocolate lab, Mocha came to us through a coworker who couldn't tolerate her digging anymore but did not want to surrender her to a shelter. She quickly became known as our "Princess" and was never seen too far from Calamity's side.

Off the four of us went to one of our favorite catfish holes. We packed in all the essentials: rods, tackle box, folding chairs, snacks, drinks, and dogs. It was a perfect evening; the temperature was just right, and a nice breeze was blowing. The dogs were enjoying themselves very much as well. We didn't catch anything at all, but we did relish our evening out. When it was time to leave, we returned the chairs to their sleeves, made sure all our trash was picked up, divided everything up, and turned to make our way back to the truck.

One problem: it was pitch black, and we had failed to bring a flashlight. Or a phone. Or anything else that might serve to illuminate our path back to civilization. We tried to make our way very carefully through the uneven and rocky terrain, but we had no way of seeing where the best footholds were.

Have no fear! Calamity and Mocha could tell we were struggling and swiftly came to the rescue. We knew they could easily find their way to the truck with their keen senses of sight and smell. So rather than relying on our poor vision to lead us out, we faithfully followed in the footsteps of the Queen and our Princess, stepping where they stepped, pausing where they paused, and eventually setting foot on solid ground right beside our trusty Dodge.

In our time of darkness and uncertainty, when we could not find our way by sight, we had no choice but to place our faith in those devoted animals who had accompanied us on our trip. According to *Merriam-Webster's Dictionary*, faith is a firm belief in something for which there is no proof. We had no proof that the dogs could get us safely home, but we knew their track record and were happy to place our faith in them. How lucky we were to have them with us when we needed them. It would have been much more difficult for us to find our way if we'd been alone.

There are times in life when we have to forego the proof and just step out to walk by faith, not by sight. Fortunately, we are never alone in this life. Our guide is always with us to show the way. But we must learn to walk by faith in him, stepping where he steps, pausing where he pauses, and believing without proof that he will direct us to the place where we can safely set our feet on solid ground.

Chapter 8

Have You Forgotten about Me?

You have searched me, Lord, and you know me. You know when I sit and when I rise; you perceive my thoughts from afar. You discern my going out and my lying down; you are familiar with all my ways. Before a word is on my tongue you, Lord, know it completely . . . Where can I go from your Spirit? Where can I flee from your presence?
—Psalm 139:1–4, 7

It wasn't too terribly long ago that a sweet baby boy crossed our threshold to begin a fresh, new life in the Simmons' household. A rather plump little Lab-mix, he was coal black with the exception of a few white hairs in the very tip of his tail, one white toe on his left rear paw, and a white, duck-shaped bib on his chest.

As soon as he set foot in the door, Bexar must have sensed he had a daunting task ahead of him. He had to establish his place in the pack, which at that time consisted of two old granny dogs, Calamity Jane and Mocha, who instantly despised him. After several months of persistence on Bexar's part, and a multitude of assurances to the girls that he wasn't going anywhere, they finally relented and accepted him as one of their own. The three dogs became one unified family.

Since his own induction four years ago, Bexar has witnessed numerous changes in his pack. He lost his matriarch, Calamity Jane; gained a new running buddy, Jayke; temporarily hosted an abandoned dog, Casper; welcomed a sister, Dixie; said a final goodbye to Mocha; and then bid farewell to Jayke, as he left us to begin the next chapter of his life with our daughter Sydney.

Needless to say, the recent arrival of Brady's puppy, Tydis, has changed the dynamic of Bexar's pack once more. He now holds the title of patriarch, top dog, responsible party. It is now up to him to help teach this youngster what acceptable canine behavior looks like. (As a side note: If you've ever owned a Weimaraner, you absolutely understand that even if the Weimaraner happened to be the oldest of all the dogs, he or she would *never* be the responsible party. It's just not in their genetics.)

Many times it appears that the majority of our family's attention is expended on Tydis and Dixie. Ty gets attention because he's a puppy and needs constant supervision, direction, and correction. And Dixie gets attention because, well, she's a Weimaraner, and needs constant supervision, direction, and correction. And we can't overlook the fact that Ty is absolutely adorable, and Dixie is gorgeous. Some might even say she is majestic. Actually, I'm probably the only one who would say this.

And then you have Bexar with all his stellar qualities. Trustworthy, reliable, and obedient, he is the polar opposite of Ty and Dixie. You would think this fine animal would have mounds of accolades heaped upon his remarkable head daily—if not hourly. Sadly, just as in families with multiple siblings, the "good dog" sometimes gets snubbed. I was reminded of this phenomenon just this morning.

After breakfast, I did a cursory cleaning of the house, then returned to the bedroom with my laptop and Bible in one hand and a steaming cup of tea in the other. Of course, the doggie procession followed closely behind. As we neared the bed, Dixie assumed her pouncing stance, preparing to hop into her assigned spot, wherever that may be. I quickly set my computer and Bible on the bed, arranging them in such a way that she would understand: "This is MY space . . . Choose your space accordingly." Before she could spring into action, Bexar launched himself onto the bed like a heat-seeking missile locked on its target. He decided to claim the corner right next to mine, which is out of character for him since that is the space Dixie usually occupies.

This impromptu modification in the normal arrangement didn't seem to faze anyone, so we settled in to do what we had gathered there to do: I would write while they slept. My word processer hadn't even fully opened yet when I felt Bexar gently lay his head on my leg and press his cheek against me. When I looked down at that innocent boy's face, I saw uncertainty reflected in his eyes. They seemed to be asking, "Have you forgotten about me? Do you remember that I am here? Can you even see me?" In that moment, I wondered if Bexar had x-ray vision and was able to see directly into my soul. Those very questions had been haunting me.

Years ago I completed a course on the *The 5 Love Languages* by Dr. Gary Chapman. I was able to confirm through those lessons what I had suspected for quite some time. The language I speak most fluently is "Acts of Service." I spend a great deal of time doing for others, and it brings me a tremendous amount of joy. I cannot begin to express how satisfied I feel when I've been able to do something that lifts the spirit of one who so desperately needs encouragement. The act doesn't have to be magnificent to be mighty. Often times, the smallest gesture has the largest effect.

That being said, my love language can occasionally wear me out to the point that I begin to wonder if this service provider is appreciated, or even acknowledged, at all. And I begin to wonder, "Have they forgotten about me? Do they remember that I am here? Can they even see me?"

Please don't misunderstand. I don't set out to perform these acts of service in an attempt to get a return on investment. These acts are sincerely done out of love and kindness, to show others that they are in my thoughts and are important to me. But when all is said and done, my human nature likes to step in and throw a little pity party. Maybe you've been there before, too. Maybe you feel that your efforts are overlooked. Maybe because you're the "good dog" in the pack, your kind acts have come to be expected and, therefore, seem to be ignored.

Here's the thing. Sometimes we do good deeds, and they go unnoticed. Sometimes we serve others and are not acknowledged. Sometimes we bend over backwards and are not appreciated. And that's okay. Because no matter who forgets about us, refuses to recognize we are here, or fails to see us when we stand right in front of them, we are always remembered and acknowledged by our heavenly Father. We always have been, and we always will be. The psalmist marveled, "You are familiar with all my ways . . . Where can I go from your spirit? Where can I flee from your presence?" Nowhere. There is absolutely nowhere we can go that God doesn't see us, acknowledge us, and love us.

Bexar's feelings of insecurity are not unlike my own. But even when it seems I have been overlooked by the ones I love most, I can rest in the assurance that I am always on the mind of the one who loves me most. I am not forgotten by my Father. Neither are you.

Chapter 9

If You're Happy and You Know It, Wag Your Tail

I know what it is to be in need, and I know what it is to have plenty. I have learned the secret of being content in any and every situation, whether well fed or hungry, whether living in plenty or in want. I can do all this through him who gives me strength.
—Philippians 4:12–13

One of thte greatest things about a movie is its soundtrack. Through the soundtrack, you are introduced to songs you may not have been inclined to hear otherwise. For instance, my musical preferences include Texas/red-dirt country, contemporary Christian, classical, and bluegrass, with a healthy dose of 80s pop thrown in. That being said, if it weren't for the release of the movie "Despicable Me 2," I may have never had the pleasure of hearing that catchy tune "Happy" by Pharrell Williams. (Actually, I think we can assume that's not true at all, since it has been heard in the background of many a meme since its release. I'm sure I would have come across it eventually.)

Regardless of how I became aware of the song, it is now an integral part of my "Fun Songs" playlist. I cannot listen to it without a vivid picture of Dixie coming to mind. You see, Dixie is by far the happiest dog I've ever known. It doesn't matter what life throws her way, she rolls with it and remains happy.

She is constantly getting into trouble, and I use the term "trouble" loosely. In all actuality, as a Weimaraner, she doesn't understand the concept of authentic trouble. What she believes she is getting into is more or less a mild form of mischief. And in the mind of a Weim, trouble and mischief are separated by a vast number of degrees. Maybe you've heard of the game, "The Six Degrees of Kevin Bacon," where you name an actor or actress and the computer links Kevin Bacon to that personality via the movies they have in common. This is to be done in as few steps as possible, preferably six "degrees" or less. Similarly, Dixie is able to link trouble to mild mischief in, say, one hundred degrees—or more. Never less. Definitely never less.

This dog has found herself lying in her time-out bed for a host of offenses, most of them involving the theft of food. For your enjoyment, I have listed a few below:

- Sneaking freshly baked muffins from the cooling rack—on three separate occasions—and eating them all (including the muffin papers)
- Chewing a hole in the zippered fabric snack bag for our beach trip and eating many of the snacks (including the plastic bags they were in)
- Pilfering a loaf of banana nut bread off the counter and eating all of it (including the plastic bag it was in)
- Stealing a summer sausage log off the island and eating all of it (including the wrapper)
- Taking a bag of dry pinto beans from the counter and attempting to eat them (and the bag they were in)

The list goes on and on, but I really don't wish to cause her further humiliation. The point is, after completing the sentence that was handed down to her for each of these wrongdoings, when released from her time-out bed, she always managed to rebound back to her typical, happy, Weimaraner self. In her mind, the past is the past, and the future is yet to be determined.

But the present? That's another story altogether. In the present, she chooses to be happy.

Happiness is easy enough when our bellies are full and we want for nothing. When we feel "like a room without a roof," being happy feels automatic. But what about when the present doesn't look so optimistic? What if it involves hunger? Or pain and suffering? It's hard to be happy in the midst of adversity. But that's exactly what the apostle Paul challenges us to do. Even he had to learn to be content— no matter what his circumstances were.

I have to remember that I was never promised days filled with sunshine and roses. On occasion, hardship and misfortune will certainly darken my door. However, the promise I can always take to heart is that no matter what my circumstances are, "I can do all this through him who gives me strength."

Chapter 10

Keep Your Eye on the Ball—or, Bird

Keep your eyes straight ahead; ignore all sideshow distractions.

—Proverbs 4:25 (MSG)

At the tender age of fifty(ish), Ken Simmons acquired something he'd wished for his entire adult life, but was never able to obtain: a bird dog. I'm talking about a bona fide hunting dog—the kind that expectantly watches the sky for birds, marks them, retrieves them, and drops them right into your eagerly awaiting hand. Yes, after much work with dove scent, rubber decoys, pistol blanks, whistles, and treats, Bexar had earned his stripes and was field ready.

When September rolled around, signifying the commencement of Bexar's first official dove season, he blew all of our minds. Not only did he retrieve the birds he'd marked for Ken while patiently listening for the command to "get the bird," he recovered all of our birds, although he hadn't even put eyes on them. This dog was a natural! Thanks to him, we ended the season with only two birds unaccounted for.

Unfortunately for Bexar, busy schedules interfered with the target practice that was necessary to prepare us for the following September, so his second season proved to be uneventful. Because we were incapable of hitting anything, his tracking skills were negatively affected. How can I be sure of this, you ask? Allow me to fast forward to the next fall, September 1, 2014.

It is not quite six o'clock in the morning and is rather dark as Ken, our oldest son Kenny, and I make our way to what we believe will be a prime location for kicking off this inaugural hunt. We are laden with folding chairs, bottled water, additional ammo, and, of course, we have Bexar and Dixie in tow.

(Let me go ahead and address your question, "Does Dixie also retrieve?" No. She does nothing of the sort. We are holding out hope that by next season she will figure it out, but at this point, she accompanies us for two reasons not even remotely related to dove hunting. First, it makes her feel like she's a part of something, something big.

Second, if we leave her alone in the house, she will destroy it. All of it. There is absolutely no question about this. Mostly, we take her with us to avoid the second scenario. There you have it, in a nutshell.)

We draw closer to a small clearing in the tree line that will comfortably accommodate our three chairs while keeping us hidden from view, and Bexar begins to get antsy. He has been here before and seems to know what is in store for him. We settle in and wait for sunrise.

As the sun starts to peek over the horizon, several other hunters converge on this particular field. A group of men in a pickup drive past us and make their way to a place a little farther south of the location we have chosen. The quartet in the truck bed is comprised of two middle aged men, an older gentleman, and a young boy; they immediately spot our dogs.

The eldest man, whom I assume to be the child's grandfather, gives him a detailed explanation of the job description for a good hunting dog, while I silently pray that Bexar won't embarrass us.

Within moments, the sun has fully risen, and the birds start flying. My husband, being the master marksman that he is, takes a shot and hits his target. Not a second is lost as Bexar races out to where he marked the bird. He is on it like a duck on a Jjune bug. Before we know it, he stands inches from the fallen dove, which has landed just a few yards in front of the inquisitive boy and his people. My heart swells with pride as I consider the impact this majestic animal's skill will have on the impressionable young lad.

Pause. Have you ever had a child who was the "go-to player" on his sports team? This child is the one who always sinks the winning basket or makes the first down or hits the line drive that lands at least one person on base when the game is on the line. He's so amazing all the time, it never once occurs to you that he might shoot a brick or fumble the ball or hit a pop fly. Never. Occurs. To. You.

Okay, resume. All eyes are on Bexar as he reaches his prize. But suddenly, a second bird appears on the scene, flying up from the ground near the fallen dove. I begin to panic, trying to assure myself that it's going to be okay. It's just a momentary distraction. He will let the flying bird go and retrieve the one he set out to find. But I am sadly mistaken. This is no momentary distraction; it has completely captured Bexar's attention so that he is no longer even aware of the existence of another bird.

Ken blows the whistle and calls Bexar back to us, but he is on a mission. He tries his best to catch the runaway dove as it flies just out of reach of those sharp canines. Running through the field in crazy-eight patterns, jumping around like a jackrabbit in an attempt to snag the bird, and stampeding through the temporary camp of his captured audience down the way, that dog not only embarrasses us, he embarrasses himself. Rather than keeping his focus on what lay straight ahead, he allows himself to be distracted, and in the process, creates his own silly sideshow! It doesn't take us long to decide there might be a better spot in the adjacent field—where no other hunters can be found.

With so many stimulating and intriguing options out there, it's easy to become distracted and lose our focus in life. We are instructed to keep our eyes straight ahead and not allow ourselves to become sidetracked by things of this world. I love the way *The Message* translation puts it: "Ignore all sideshow distractions." Do you sometimes look around and feel like you're in one of the three rings of a circus, surrounded by sideshow distractions? I sure do!

Our hunting fiasco with Bexar reminds me of the importance of keeping my focus straight ahead and ignoring all sideshow distractions. They will only pull me away from my true purpose in life and will likely turn *me* into a special kind of sideshow in the process!

Chapter 11

When You Grow Old,
I Will Carry You

*Even to your old age and gray hairs I am he, I am
he who will sustain you. I have made you and I will
carry you; I will sustain you and I will rescue you.*
—Isaiah 46:4

When the topic of conversation turns to canine companions, invariably the word "loyal" is heard. Over the years, we have had the distinct pleasure of sharing our home with some extremely amazing dogs. One of those sweet babies was Calamity Jane, "the Queen."

She was a black Chow mix and was rescued from an animal shelter at the age of one-and-a-half years. Ken brought her home shortly after she had undergone hip surgery following a car accident, hence the name "Calamity" Jane. Of all the energetic, healthy animals confined in that shelter, he chose the one he felt most needed to be rescued. As he carried her over the threshold and into the Simmons' home, she had no way of knowing she had just hit pay dirt.

Once she became a member of the family, Calamity had to learn the same lessons taught to all Simmons' pets, lessons founded on firm boundaries and loving discipline. Ken knew these guidelines would not only produce an obedient dog, they would also provide a hedge of protection around her, keeping her safe. Certainly there were times it was difficult to correct her misconduct, even in love. But in the end, her training paid off, and she flourished into one of the most submissive, trustworthy, and loyal dogs we have ever known.

Calamity's reconstructed hip never seemed to slow her down. As a matter of fact, if Ken had owned cattle when Calamity came on the scene, she would have made a fantastic herding dog. But, alas, he did not. So instead she had to hone her instincts by terrorizing two Egyptian goats. Try as they might, there was no way they could get around her. She would cut them off and redirect them before they even knew what had happened. She was a boss.

Sadly, not all of our memories of Calamity are fond ones. Ken recalls relaxing in his recliner one afternoon, watching some TV (probably "through the backside of his eyelids," as my dad would have said) when Calamity entered the room and silently took a seat on the floor beside him. He instinctively reached down to pet her and discovered she was wet. Upon further inspection, he realized that she was actually bleeding.

We live in a rural area and our dogs spend a good bit of time outdoors. They never wander off too far and generally come back quickly when called. On this particular day, Calamity had ventured a little too far away from the house and had been hit by a car, for the second time in her short life. The impact knocked her collar off. It was found several yards away from the house in the middle of the road. She suffered from a serious case of road rash and required a good deal of stitches. One of her canine teeth was broken off at the gum line and had to be surgically removed. The worst tragedy was that her beautiful Chow tail was fractured and required complete amputation. Perhaps Ken should have considered changing her name to something a little more optimistic after her adoption. Things that make you go, "Hmmm. . ."

Fortunately, Calamity made a full recovery and never strayed too far from Ken's side after that. She recognized him as her protector, her rescuer, her savior. There was absolutely no question that she completely and wholly belonged to him. She was as hopelessly devoted to Ken as he was to her.

As the years passed, Calamity began to show her age. Her muzzle turned from black to gray to white, and she developed a mass on one of her rear legs. A visit to the vet confirmed our worst fears: cancer. In order to ensure her comfort, we were told the tumor needed to be removed. However, he could make no guarantee that the growth would not return. The surgery was scheduled, the mass removed, and the Queen sent home to recuperate.

Just as the doctor predicted, the tumor returned. Not once, but twice more, Calamity underwent surgery in an attempt to rid her body of the cancer that was trying so hard to steal her away from us. When the mass resurfaced for the fourth time, we knew we would soon have to make a heart-wrenching decision.

Although her mind remained keen and sharp, her body was steadily growing weaker. The mass on her leg made walking problematic. Ultimately, Ken had to carry her outside to relieve herself in the morning, if she hadn't already done so during the night. With each passing day, her quality of life, as well as her dignity, diminished. The moment for the tragic decision had finally come.

One last time, Ken gathered the Queen into his arms and carried her out of the house. En route to the vet's office, Calamity Jane was showered with hugs and kisses and assurances that she would be sorely missed by each and every one of us. Then, at the appointed time, surrounded by her family and sprinkled with tears, she breathed her last.

Even to her old age and gray hairs, Ken did his best to carry, sustain, and rescue Calamity, this companion that had held such a tender spot in his heart for thirteen years. Over the course of Calamity's life, her way had become challenging, her burden hard to bear. She needed a champion, a hero.

This life does not always offer us a nice, even, paved road to travel. Sometimes the way is hard, and we are met with calamities of our own—maybe more than just once or twice. But even to our old age and gray hairs, there is one who sustains us. The very one who created us keeps us under his constant watch and stands ready to rescue us. God wants to be our champion and our hero, if only we will allow him.

Chapter 12

Kindness Counts

Be kind and compassionate to one another, forgiving each other, just as in Christ God forgave you.
—Ephesians 4:32

Not all days are red-letter, gold star, "Attagirl!" kinds of days. Some are more like lumps of coal, sack of rocks, "Way to go, loser!" kinds of days. This day started out as one of the latter.

On this proverbial roller coaster called life, it would appear we are now plummeting along the downhill side of one of the ride's larger arcs. It feels as if we've solely been going up and down for quite some time, experiencing no twists or turns and detecting no directional changes. If I didn't know any better, I might think I was unwittingly participating in the movie "A Series of Unfortunate Events".

Okay, you're right. I'm probably making it sound much worse than it actually is. Each of us has our own set of circumstances to deal with on a daily basis, and those circumstances seem to be ever changing. I have no reason to think I should be an exception to this unwritten rule, so the degree of harm these events have inflicted on my cheery disposition is no excuse for my behavior this morning.

On earlier pages, I have briefly alluded to the tendency of our Weimaraner, Dixie, to have a mind of her own and to exercise her free will with reckless abandon. In fact, she chose to do just that this very morning.

We are finally coming into some cooler temperatures here in North Texas and have actually been blessed with a little rain to boot. Rain always brings me mixed emotions. On the one hand, it's great for greening up the yard, popping out those pretty, purple sage blooms, and contributing to a greater pecan crop. On the other hand, it makes for a nasty, muddy mess on the tile when we let the dogs back in from doing their business. It's not really even a problem unless they decide to run into the bedroom and hop onto the bed—which, incidentally, has a fresh, new quilt on it that yours truly recently completed. I think maybe you're starting to pick up what I'm putting down.

This morning, while the dogs were finishing up breakfast, I started my Monday morning damage control from a weekend of being lazy and doing nothing but being lazy and doing nothing. Upon request, I let the dogs out to take care of business. When they came back in the house, I told them in no uncertain terms not to get on the bed. Bexar and Ty obediently complied; however, Dixie, being a Weimaraner, did not. Her inner voice spoke loud and clear when it said, "Sure! Go ahead. Get on the bed." Not once, not twice, but three times she disobeyed me, and three times she was scolded.

By her fourth attempt, I had lost it. I banned her from the bedroom altogether. In a loud, angry voice that I'm not sure she has ever heard me use, I commanded her to get out and go to the living room. Her response communicated to me that she felt stunned, fearful, and confused. Instead of hastily leaving the bedroom, she skulked away from me and lay down on her own bed beside ours, making herself as slight as possible. She did just the opposite of leaving the bedroom—she got settled in for a long stay! I could feel the irritation boiling up inside me. But, wait. Was I angry at Dixie for disobeying my initial request not to get on the bed? Or was I angry at her for defying me by refusing to go into the living room? I didn't really care what the reason was because it was irrelevant right now. I had a point to prove, and I was on a mission to prove it: "I'm in charge here, and when I say do something, you jolly well better do it."

Continuing to use a tone of voice that was less than gentle, I dragged her off her bed and into the living room where she promptly ran to the other dog bed and lay down, again making herself very small. Leaving her, I returned to the bedroom to finish cleaning.

As I worked through my to-do list in silence, it only took a moment for me to realize the true source of my anger. My feelings of doubt, uncertainty, insecurity, and even abandonment relating to the issues we've been dealing with lately had finally surfaced. And those emotions, along with the circumstances that led to them, made me mad. The only thing Dixie had done was make herself available to incur my wrath when the feelings of disappointment finally surfaced.

Ashamed, I walked slowly to the bedroom door that leads into the living room and called Dixie's name. She hopped up and ran straight to me. We walked into the bedroom, and I sat down on the bed. She did not join me until I patted the mattress and extended the invitation. I apologized to her for my horrible behavior and for making her bear the brunt of my angry outburst. I asked for her forgiveness, and my apology was met with wonderfully sweet kisses, all over my face. Her forgiveness was instantaneous. She didn't even need all the words I delivered as we sat together. She knew as soon as I called her name that I was sorry for what I had done, and she sat at the ready to forgive.

God commanded us to be kind and compassionate to one another. I showed Dixie no kindness or compassion as I went on my rampage sparked by self-pity. Although I didn't deserve it, Dixie offered me unwavering forgiveness, somewhat like the forgiveness we receive from God, through Jesus Christ. He knows that we seek forgiveness as soon as we call his name, and he sits at the ready to forgive. His unfailing love and immediate forgiveness are always available to us, if we will but ask.

Chapter 13

No Fighting!

Then the Lord said to Cain, "Why are you angry? Why is your face downcast? If you do what is right, will you not be accepted? But if you do not do what is right, sin is crouching at your door; it desires to have you, but you must rule over it."

—Genesis 4:6–7

There is something fascinating about an individual who has the ability to alter permanently the behavior of animals. Take famous dog trainer Cesar Milan, for example. Our family has been known to waste entire afternoons watching back to back episodes of "The Dog Whisperer." (Thank you, Netflix, for stealing away entire days of my life that I can never get back.) By now we can pretty safely determine which pets will be trained on their home turf and which ones will be taken on an extended field trip for training with Cesar's pack.

Some dogs are naturally more submissive than others, and some are naturally more dominant. In a pack environment, most animals determine their place in the pecking order fairly quickly. If you have ever watched Cesar introduce a new dog to his pack, you have undoubtedly noted it is done slowly and deliberately. The visitor is brought through the gate, given the opportunity to familiarize itself with the new surroundings, and then the dogs do the rest. Cesar's pack is so well established, with every animal confident in its position, that no one feels intimidated by the newcomer. And so, in turn, no one feels the need to threaten the guest.

However, when you introduce a young, somewhat dominant female dog into a small, slightly unstable pack, you can expect to have some issues. Or at least that's what we expected when Dixie entered our world.

It seems we always have a pack of dogs. We can't be satisfied with only one. There's far too much love in this house to be limited to only one animal. It is our fear that lavishing such massive quantities of affection on one dog could result in canine implosion, which we are certain would be messy, at best. And who wants to risk that? So to prevent this from happening, we try to maintain a ratio of at least one human for every dog.

At the time of Dixie's arrival, we were a little off on our count. Ken had three-year-old Bexar, Sydney had two-year-old Jayke, and we'll say Brady and I shared "Grandma" Mocha. We were clearly short one dog, but luckily for us, my youngest sister had a canine crisis on her hands that I was sure we could solve.

(As a side note, Dixie's original name was Pixie. That is a precious name for a sweet, little, blue-eyed, floppy-eared, grey-ghost baby girl raised in the city and taken to dog parks to play. But because I love my husband and couldn't bear the thought of him out in the field, clad in camo, toting a shotgun and hollering for "Pixie" to retrieve his birds, I opted to change her name to Dixie. I believe this is a good, strong, southern name that a man can use in the field without fear of ridicule.)

With my nephews, two very young boys, Dixie's high energy level, constant desire to play, and demand for attention were proving to be too much for Amy and her family. These characteristics also caused us some concern over how she would adapt to our pack. She was only eight months old at the time, still very much a pup, and we had two fairly young dogs and one very old dog at home. For the first time, I began to wonder if acquiring another dog was a good idea or not. This was going to require a great deal of serious consideration. It took about seven minutes of deliberation to reach our verdict. There were basically only two factors that influenced our decision to adopt Dixie: (1) thanks to William Wegman and Sesame Street, I have been in love with Weimaraners for a very long time, and (2) Ken Simmons has a hard time telling me no unless it's absolutely necessary.

Just before Thanksgiving, I brought Dixie home to meet the other dogs. Our biggest concern was how she would react to Jayke, since they were both so young. We decided to give her a few days to get used to her new surroundings before introducing the two of them. In the meantime, we allowed her to have supervised access to both Mocha and Bexar, which seemed to go pretty well.

When the time came to insert Jayke into the picture, we leashed both dogs, held our breath, said a prayer, and let the sniffing commence. It didn't take long for Dixie to begin to demonstrate some pretty dominant behaviors, which, in turn, made Jayke slightly uncomfortable. Each time she behaved inappropriately, she was reprimanded.

My husband, like Cesar Milan, has the ability to cause animals to want to be obedient, which makes interacting with them a pleasant experience. Throughout his life, he has successfully trained horses, dogs, and children by adhering to one simple principle: make the right thing easy and the wrong thing hard. When Dixie did the right thing by correctly responding to cues and commands, she was praised and given a treat. When she displayed the wrong behavior, either by showing aggression toward the other dogs or by refusing to follow instructions, she was appropriately disciplined.

True to her breed, Dixie is a very intelligent dog. The reason Weimaraners tend to get a bad rap is that they need constant stimulation or they will become bored. And when they become bored, they can become quite destructive. Her training, both on- and off-leash, offered a challenging workout for her brain, and she rose to the occasion. Only in rare instances did our personal belongings suffer damage as a result of her boredom. She also seemed to have found her place in the pack, outranked by Mocha and Bexar, but not quite as low on the totem pole as Jayke. However, she just couldn't shake the feeling that maybe she could trump Bexar, too.

There were a few instances where she tried to assert her dominance over Bexar, and each time, Ken allowed him to respond naturally, as he would in a pack that had no human involvement. He was tolerant of her first couple of assaults, but when she had pushed him too far, he made it clear that her behavior was unacceptable and inappropriate. Her response was immediate. She quickly backed away, shaking her head in disbelief as if to say, "Hey, wait a minute. What was that all about? He isn't supposed to treat me like that!"

Because Dixie willingly chose to do the wrong thing, Bexar had to teach her the unpleasant consequences that result from poor choices. If you recall, every time she performed a correct action, she was rewarded and given the opportunity to enjoy some well-deserved time on easy street. She had already demonstrated her ability to distinguish between behaviors that were right and wrong, just as she had determined her true place in the pack, between Bexar and Jayke. Acknowledging that role would certainly lead to acceptance by the other dogs, but more than once, she chose to do the wrong thing, which made assimilation into the pack more difficult than it needed to be.

Dixie has been with us for just shy of a year at this writing and has come such a long way. She is still considered a puppy and has much to learn. The story of Dixie's introduction to our pack is my reminder that we are constantly faced with choices. Sin crouches at our door, desiring to have control over us. But if we want to be accepted by God, we must always choose to do what is right.

Chapter 14

Quick to Listen,
Slow to Speak

My dear brothers and sisters, take note of this: Everyone should be quick to listen, slow to speak and slow to become angry, because human anger does not produce the righteousness that God desires.
—James 1:19–20

When I was very young, I was given a nickname that has stuck with me through the years. Actually, it wasn't just given to me. I earned it. I worked hard for it. There was no doubt in the mind of anyone who met me why I was referred to by this name.

Those of you who are around my age will recall a cartoon character who went by the name of Sniffles. (If you are a youngster unfortunate enough not to be familiar with Sniffles, please put the book down briefly and consult Google.) Yes, that adorable little mouse with his cheery face, pigeon toes, and tiny little hat—and incessant talking—was an animated favorite. Oh, that mouse never shut up. Or, breathed much, as I recall. He'd pause for just one huge breath between never-ending strings of words.

Yes, I was affectionately known in my home and surrounding circles as "Sniffles." At that age, I had such a cheery face, sometimes stood pigeon toed when I was really attempting to pour on the innocent act, and enjoyed wearing a cowboy hat. However, those are not the reasons I got the nickname. Quite honestly, I never knew when to shut up.

Things haven't changed much as I've gotten older. I've just resorted to writing some of those words down instead of speaking them. Now, Ken Simmons is another story altogether. He's more the strong, silent type, but not necessarily because he doesn't enjoy conversing. More times than not, it's because he can't get a word in edgewise, especially when our daughters or my mom and sisters are involved in the conversation. Poor, sweet husband of mine!

Ken is actually a brilliant conversationalist. Around these parts, he's kind of like E.F. Hutton—when Ken speaks, everybody listens! But that is because he does the same when we talk. He is quick to listen and slow to speak.

And true to the wisdom imparted in the book of James, he is also slow to become angry.

When Ken and I were just dating, he did quite a bit of hunting. In his absence on the weekends, I would pack up my kids and head out to the sticks to house-sit and take care of the animals. It was kind of like a mini road trip to the country for us, always full of fun and adventure for a carload of city folk. My, how times have changed!

Usually, the "animals" consisted of Seminole, the quarter horse, Calamity Jane, and Molly. Now of all the dogs who have crossed my path, Molly was definitely the most unique. Several years ago, Nick (Ken's youngest) spent the night with a friend and came home with a new puppy, sort of a parting sleepover prize, you might say. Nick apparently took one look at Molly and decided she needed to be his dog. So, as any innocent boy would do, he asked the question all parents hear eventually, "Can I keep her?"

The unique thing about Molly was her face. We aren't sure what happened to her, but when we speak of her, we refer to her in a variety of ways: "She looks like Jimmy Durante." (Again, youngsters: Google.) Or, "She looks like someone hit her in the face with a frying pan." She was by no means a contender for Best of Show, or even Best of Breed. But that sweet angel had a heart of gold and would go to great lengths to be with her people.

On more than one occasion, she joined us for a day at the lake. She was at least part Labrador retriever and, therefore, loved being at the lake. She had a blast playing by herself, in and out of the water, swimming and running, shaking and sunning. That is, she was happy unless the kids were enjoying a swim. Then she wasn't content to be by herself. Every time she saw one of their heads dip below lake level, she rushed to the rescue. It was as if she thought the child was in distress, drowning. Of course, all were fine—until she arrived. In her frantic effort to save the victim, the rescuer came very close to drowning him herself! But the kids just laughed at her attempts, understanding that she just wanted to make sure they were not in danger, so she could spend more time by their side.

In the early years of Molly and Nick, as with most dogs and their boys, they were inseparable. This, of course, meant that Molly shared Nick's bed at night. This was the only bed she was allowed to be on, since Ken Simmons has always had a hard and fast rule of no dogs on the bed. Well, he used to have that rule. It's true what they say: "love conquers all."

As I said earlier, Molly was a people pleaser. She wanted nothing more than to be close to her people. In the same room was good, but in the same bed was "bedder." (Yes, that just happened.) On my house-sitting weekends, she would start out on the floor, usually with her head resting on the window ledge, staring out the window, watching for anything out of the ordinary so she would be ready to protect her people in an instant.

As time passed, she would make her first attempt at hopping onto the bed, which would be met with a firm, "Molly! No!" and a return to the floor. Molly loved this game, so we would play it many times before I would eventually fall asleep. Once slumber had me, she knew I was powerless to prevent her from getting on the bed. So I would awake in the mornings with that super-sweet, jacked-up face staring at me. I couldn't be angry. She just wanted me to know how much she cared about me and my safety through the long, dark night.

Typically, on house-sitting weekends, we had no plans and were able to arrive on Friday afternoon and stay put til Sunday evening. On one weekend in particular, Sydney had an activity with her 4-H Club that we needed to attend. We knew the event would last around four hours, and it was a nice afternoon, so we decided to put Calamity and Molly on the screened-in porch while we were gone.

They acted as if this was normal practice, and we were on our way. At the event, we learned how to make flour tortillas and tamales. (Like I said, we needed to attend this activity. As in, it was imperative that we attend this activity. It's a Texas thing, y'all!) After we'd mastered these coveted culinary skills, we loaded up our goodies and returned to Valley View.

If you've ever watched Madeline with your young girls, you are familiar with Miss Clavel's keen sense of awareness when things aren't "quite right." Well, this gal's got her own keen senses, and let me tell you, the moment I saw the big hole in the screen and Molly on the other side of it, I immediately knew something wasn't quite right.

Sydney and I exchanged worried looks. What would Ken say when he got home the next day? How angry would he be? Would he shake his finger at us and raise his voice and say, "You had *one* job!" (I would find out later that due to the odd size of the screens on the porch, the material needed was special order only. Yikes.) We had to think quickly. We hopped back in the car, leaving the dogs in the house this time, and dashed to Lowe's to get screen material to make repairs. If nothing else, we could patch the holes until we were able to order new screens.

We put our best foot forward and got to work. We cut patches out of the new, non-matching screen material and used thin wire to "stitch" them to the existing, mangled screens. It wasn't pretty, but it was all we could do on such short notice. If only Molly had destroyed the screens on Friday instead!

We waited on pins and needles for the blue Dodge to pull into the driveway, and when it did, our hearts began to race. The moment of truth had arrived, and we were nervous. Ken and I had been dating for a fairly short time, during which I could not recall ever seeing him angry. I had no idea what kind of reaction to expect, so I braced for the worst.

After a quick kiss and exchange of pleasantries, I mentioned that we'd had a bit of an unfortunate event over the weekend and led him to the porch. He gave the screens a quick glance as he intently listened to my account of how we came to be in this situation. Then he took Molly outside, and directing her attention to the damage she had done, gently rebuked her for this misconduct. He did not yell or hit, scream or kick; he reprimanded her while maintaining a calm and assertive demeanor.

Molly's body language told us she heard the message, loud and clear, even though it was anything but loud. With ears back, head down, body low, and eyes cast tentatively toward Ken's face as he spoke, it was obvious she knew she had made a wrong choice. She had been left in a semi-secure place while her people had gone elsewhere, without her. She was compelled to find them, so she could be close to them once again.

I stood amazed in the presence of this man's calmness. When I expressed my awe at his self-control, his response immediately deepened my love for him. After all, you can tell a lot about a man by the way he treats his dogs. "They're screens, babe. They can be replaced," he said. "Molly was just being a dog, doing what dogs do." Quick to listen. Slow to speak. Slow to become angry.

So often I find myself in situations that make me angry. And I'm not talking about righteous anger here; I'm talking everyday anger. You know the kind: you're in the middle of a recipe and reach for the milk, only to find a scant tablespoon has been left in the carton and returned to the fridge; your teenage son voluntarily offers to clean out the barn and in the process of pulling the truck inside manages to add his own brand of East Texas pinstripes to both sides of the bed; your daughter takes the car to fill it up for you but forgets to return the radio to the "old people" station so when you get in again, the bass is thumping so loudly you can't even get your brain to function long enough to find the power button.

These are such minor infractions, but they have the ability to make me very angry. My initial reaction is always to lash out, to let everyone know how frustrated I am at that moment. I don't want to hear the offender's excuses. I want to hear—what? What do I really want to hear? My own voice blasting those I love because they committed a minor infraction? Of course not. "Because human anger does not produce the righteousness that God desires." In those times that action is necessary, choosing to listen to the offender and process his information before speaking is the better choice. If I slow down my instinct to react in anger and, instead, gently rebuke in a state of calm assertiveness, I'll have less to regret.

We live in a world full of people who are, obviously, only human. And like Molly, sometimes they will make wrong choices that will cause some sort of damage—whether to our homes, our relationships, or our lives in other ways. We must slow down our response. Be quick to listen to the reason behind their actions. Be slow to respond to the information we receive and even slower to let anger control our reaction.

Chapter 15

Things That Go Bump in the Night

The Lord does not look at the things man looks at. People look at the outward appearance, but the Lord looks at the heart.
—I Samuel 16:7

Several years ago, and for a very brief period of time, we had a little brown dachshund named Bruiser. We love the irony of giving a small dog a big name. We chose this name because when we inherited Bruiser, we already had a well-trained family dog. Samson was a purebred boxer we acquired as a pup that had grown into the finest canine specimen known to mankind. When he stood in our front yard, assessing his domain, he looked absolutely majestic.

The little dachshund had such a friendly disposition and an extremely calm demeanor, we knew a "bruiser" he would never be. On the other hand, when you introduce an easily excitable ankle-biter that fearlessly passes right under Sam's belly (and sometimes even tries to jump over his back), the decision to dub that little dynamo "Bruiser" becomes a no-brainer.

Those two looked completely ridiculous together. Seriously folks, they could have made a Kibbles 'n Bits commercial. We would take them out for walks, and everyone wanted to meet them: Samson being such a gentle giant and Bruiser such a gnat. Their introductions were always met with howls of laughter at the witty monikers we had assigned them.

But Bruiser's name wasn't the only thing that brought laughter into our lives. This guy was so cute! He just wanted to play, play, play all the time. Sitting still was not an option for anyone in our household. Bruiser believed we were to be at his beck and call twenty-four hours a day, seven days a week. Let me give you an example. Kimberly, my oldest, would get his attention and then run from him, all through the house, upstairs and down. Then she would find an empty room and stand motionless against a wall. Bruiser would find her and try to engage her in further play, but she refused to move. He'd bark and jump and spin around at her feet until she finally cracked, rolling on the floor, laughing.

Other times he would get so excited he would just run figure eights through the living room and kitchen, using the couch and the island as his anchor points. As if the sudden bursts of energy weren't enough to bring us to tears, as he transitioned from carpet to tile, his little feet would slide out from under him. But he didn't let that stop him, no sir. He kept right on running until he eventually lost all control and slid into the cabinets, or the refrigerator, or the open pantry. We slid into a coma from laughing so hard.

His greatest act of comedy, however, was not a result of something he did, but rather something that did him. It was a weekday morning, and we were rushing around trying to get everyone ready for work and school. As we were just about to sit down for breakfast, one of the kids asked, "What's wrong with Bruiser's face?" We turned to look at him, totally unprepared for what we would see. He was almost beyond recognition, his face completely covered in large bumps with hardly any space at all between them. His eyes were practically swollen shut.

At some point during the night, Bruiser had gotten into something that caused an allergic reaction. The multitude of bumps is how his body responded to it. The cause remains a mystery to this day. A quick call to the vet gave us an immediate treatment plan and the promise of an afternoon call to check on him. Once we knew he was out of danger, the humor of his predicament set in. Imagine a squirrel with a pecan held snugly in each cheek.

If Bruiser was a squirrel with seventy-five cheeks, evenly distributed over his entire head, and one oversized pecan stuffed in each cheek—well, you get the idea. That's when the laughter came, *hard*.

I can attest to the fact that he certainly wasn't pretty that morning. But it really didn't matter what he looked like on the outside, because we knew there was still a silly, playful pup on the inside that we dearly loved.

Our reaction to Bruiser is not unlike the response we have toward people we come into contact with every day. It is in our nature to base the worth of others on their outward appearance: dazzling smile, stylish haircut, trendy clothes, expensive car, and the list goes on and on. However, our humanness prevents us from seeing the intentions of the heart, which is where true value is determined. There is so much more to all of us than what can be seen by mere mortal eyes.

Seeing Bruiser's barely recognizable, puffed-up face brought a valuable lesson to light. He looked terrible. He was temporarily deformed. But he was a spunky little ball of energy that brought laughter to our entire household on a daily basis. By looking only at the outside when choosing whom to invest my time in, I risk missing out on knowing some of God's most remarkable creations. Pretty wrapping doesn't guarantee an appealing gift inside the box. Don't forget, looks can often be very deceiving.

Chapter 16

The Apple of Her Eye

Keep me as the apple of Your eye; Hide me under the shadow of Your wings.
—Psalm 17:8 (NKJV)

When we bring a new pet into our home, one of the first things we do is ensure there will be no unwanted litters of puppies in our future. It's just something we feel very strongly about. Over the years, I have often heard an owner say he doesn't want to spay his dog: "She's a woman; she needs to have at least one litter of babies."

There are several issues I have with that comment. First, while the dog is certainly female, she is not a woman. Believe me, my husband accuses me on a regular basis of humanizing our dogs, so I understand when people consider their pets to be family members. But regardless of how we treat them, dogs will never be human. Second, every female dog does not *need* to become pregnant. Imagine all the puppies living at the pound. (John Lennon could have added a stanza to "Imagine," addressing the rise in the number of shelter dogs.) Third, research has shown, and many veterinarians agree, that spaying a dog before her first heat cycle decreases her chances of developing mammary cancer by 98%.[1] That statistic alone is reason enough to have female dogs spayed before they reach six months of age.

However, I can see why a person whose dog has a natural disposition for nurturing would like to see that dog deliver at least one litter of pups. It's not about the sweetness of tiny tails, squeaky cries, and puppy breath. It's about witnessing the intense bond between the mama and her little ones. All my life I have been led to believe that being a wonderful mother comes naturally in the animal kingdom. But I've often had my doubts.

I can honestly tell you that from the time Dixie came into our home, I never once regretted the fact that she was no longer a puppy-making machine. Her

---

1   American Animal Hospital, Randolph, NJ, http://americananimalhospital.com/about-us/index.php.

original owner had the foresight to have her spayed before she went through her first heat cycle. Thank the good Lord!

Believe me when I say she is one of the finest specimens of her breed, meeting all the requirements of a show-quality canine. She is absolutely gorgeous and would, no doubt, make beautiful babies. So why am I not curious to see what kind of mom she would be?

Dixie is what we call "sketchy." She can be a little unpredictable. For instance, she sometimes growls at visitors *while they are petting her.* She wants the attention, but isn't really sure how she feels about strangers being in her house. She will roll onto her back for belly rubs, submitting totally to the caresses, then suddenly jump to her feet and run wildly around the room and onto the bed, where she collapses and waits for more tummy strokes. Once, shortly after we got her, she went from standing in the kitchen to standing on the countertop, *in a single bound.* If I were writing an alphabet book about dog breeds, W would be for "weird Weimaraners." That's really all I can say.

So when I would look at her and try to imagine six to eight puppies surrounding her, a vision of some sort of sketchy behavior with the littles would immediately flash before my eyes and cause me to shake my head and just walk away.

That is, until Tydis came along. His arrival changed everything about the way I perceived Dixie's motherly instincts.

In light of the disturbing images I conjured up in my head, you can understand the uneasiness I felt about Brady bringing a puppy into the house not too long ago. I was a nervous wreck when we introduced Dixie and Ty, but my fears have slowly diminished as they spend more and more time together, creating a bond that will see them through the many years ahead.

Although Brady has ownership of Ty in all respects, Dixie has claimed him as her very own. He has become the apple of her eye. Rarely does she let him out of her sight. If he goes to one of the dog beds to catch a nap, she is quick to follow, spooning with him as they share an afternoon siesta.

Ty's infancy makes him oblivious to Bexar's distaste for him. He will spy Bexar lying on the tile floor, cooling off after a hard day of protecting the family. Bexar's quiet state is Ty's cue to trot over and start pawing at the bigger dog in an attempt to engage him in play. Bexar typically responds with a low, warning growl, which, in turn, signals Dixie to intervene.

Like any good mama, no matter where she is or what she is doing, she leaps to her feet and runs to Ty's aid. Standing firmly between the two boys, her message is loud and clear: "Harm one hair on this puppy, and you will live to regret it."

She responds similarly when one of us has to reprimand Ty for unacceptable behavior. Although she doesn't actually step between us, she stands close by to make sure things don't escalate to a level she is uncomfortable with.

I see now that Dixie would have made a fantastic mother. I have actually seen her stand over Ty to prevent him from what she perceived to be a dangerous situation. When I try to imagine her surrounded by a litter of pups, a very different vision floods my mind these days. She would tuck each one of those babies in close, and as if she had wings, she would hide them in her shadow.

In the midst of my daily distractions, I forget that I am the apple of his eye, his precious daughter. He looks at little ol' insignificant me and smiles. (Sometimes I bet he even busts a gut laughing!) When I feel alone or afraid, God wants only to gather me to him, hide me in the shadow of his wings, and keep me safe.

Chapter 17

A Veritable Dancing Machine

To everything there is a season, a time for every purpose under heaven: a time to weep, and a time to laugh; a time to mourn, and a time to dance.
—Ecclesiastes 3:1, 4 (NKJV)

After my parents were married, they set roots in North Texas. Although they moved around within that general area, they never strayed too far outside its geographical boundaries. While serving in Arlington, they befriended a remarkable group of people that they would always refer to simply as "Our Gang."

The gang was comprised of several couples of varying ages who acted as mentors to Mom and Dad. These older and wiser men and women schooled my parents on ministry and marriage, family and finances, and just about everything in between. Although several members of the gang have since left this earth, the survivors still stay in touch to this very day.

Growing up, I have vivid memories of the gang gathered in our living room for an evening of food, fellowship, and fun. And these guys knew how to have fun. There were always games on the agenda. One game in particular was called, "Smile If You Love Me." One person would be "it," while all the others sat in a circle around him/her. The person in the center had to approach each seated guest and, using every ounce of theatrics he could muster, recite the line, "Smile if you love me," in such a way that the seated person would do just that within a predetermined period of time. The object, of course, was to keep from smiling, regardless of the tactics used to sway you otherwise. I know it sounds a little hokey, but add it to the lineup at your next gathering, and you will see for yourself how much fun it is.

When I look at the ways Tydis makes me smile, I can't help but think he would win the prize for garnering the quickest smile. I can't imagine anyone who could resist the puppy's efforts to put a smile on his face.

First of all, he's just plain adorable! His markings are enough to make me grin. That little black saddle on his back and those cute black ears with just a touch of white on them are hard to resist. And who could overlook those little black "capris" it looks like he's wearing?

And his sudden bursts of energy throughout the day definitely cause me to chuckle. He will spot Dixie lying on the living room floor, minding her own business, and decide to make his move. He jumps from the recliner, landing squarely on Dixie's midsection, then runs for his life! His route takes him behind the recliner, into the kitchen, around the island, between the coffee table and couch, and back into the living room. He comes to a screeching halt right in front of his victim with his head down and tail up, wagging out of control, as if it will fall off at any moment. Then he starts the process all over again.

But the thing that really gets me rolling is bath time. He's not a fan of bath time. He hates the confinement of the sink or tub and only tolerates the shower. But we can't ignore the obvious: he's a dog that spends a good deal of time outdoors, transforming him into a smelly dog that needs a bath.

His pitiful puppy lament begins as we struggle with getting him into the sink or tub we have chosen to use. Even though he's a small dog, sometimes it helps to have two people participate in bath time. Eventually, his cries stop, and he gives up the fight so we can commence the washing and rinsing.

This is where it gets good. As we drain the water and pull out the towel, he apparently knows it's almost over, that he's no longer a dirty, smelly dog, but instead is clean and carries the slight scent of fresh-cut flowers. And he cannot contain his excitement! We pretty much release him into the kitchen and then stand back. Way back.

He twirls and whirls and jumps for joy. I've never seen such a small dog leap so high. He runs through the house at top speed, slipping and sliding, slowing down only to change direction. Then he stops suddenly, as if someone hit the pause button. He stands completely still for a few seconds before the play button is pushed, and he gets right back to it. We get a solid five minute dance show before his energy is zapped, and he falls onto his bed, exhausted—clean, but exhausted.

There are seasons of life we all will experience: love and hate; gain and loss; life and death. We must take the good with the bad, but God doesn't want us to stay buried in bitterness, loss, or grief. While there may be a time for those things, there is also a time to accept God's peace and allow ourselves to laugh again—and even to dance.

For the most part, though, I've found that stubbornness typically leads to hurt feelings, missteps, stumbling, and often, bruised pride—and sometimes worse consequences.

I remember when I was first introduced to this country way of life. I loved watching Ken as he ground worked Seminole. Ken would slip on Sem's halter, clip the lunge line to it, and walk him out into an area of wide-open pasture. He would start by walking close to Seminole, the horse's head even with Ken's shoulder. First they would walk forward, then backward, changing direction or stopping altogether. The goal was for Seminole to follow Ken's lead closely, regardless of the horse's desires.

Then Ken would step farther away from Sem, using the lunge line to cue him on the direction he should walk. Usually things went very well, with Sem following the cues like a champ. But a few times, I saw firsthand how a strong, stubborn streak can make you stumble in a big way.

One time in particular, when Ken went out to work with Sem, it quickly became apparent that our horse had other plans in mind for how he wished to spend his evening. He was having no part of his training, firmly planting his hoof down and refusing to participate.

In addition to being dubbed a "dog whisperer," Ken is pretty good with horses. He understands that in training a horse, you must end the session on a positive note. Sure, he could let Sem off the hook and not work him that evening, but before he could call it quits for the night, Sem would have to respond favorably to one command.

He led Seminole out to the open area in the pasture and began to run him in circles. Again, Seminole chose to answer with stubbornness. After gaining a little bit of speed, he decided to show Ken who was boss. He put on the brakes and began to back up, very quickly.

Did I mention he's a quarter horse and has that enormous back end that is characteristic of the quarter horse? Well, let's just say the magnitude of junk in his trunk caused him to gain a great deal of momentum rapidly.

The wreck only took a few seconds, start to finish, but from my viewpoint, it seemed like an eternity. As if in slow motion, I watched this massive animal take a few quick steps backward, planting his back hooves firmly in the ground. Simultaneously, he reared up in front while sitting down in back, and the momentum carried him over.

You haven't seen head over heels until you've seen it carried out by a twelve hundred pound animal. He recovered quickly, getting to his feet and shaking the dirt off his back. Ken was unrattled, his focus firmly fixed on the task at hand. He quietly turned his back to Sem who, undoubtedly feeling somewhat foolish, awkwardly began making his way to Ken's shoulder. Once his head reached its appointed spot, Ken began his ground work again, and this time Sem was all too happy to join in.

After a few quick exercises with favorable responses from Seminole, Ken released him from his training. But what a peaceful session we could have all enjoyed if Sem's stubbornness hadn't caused him to stumble.

When we choose to follow God's laws and walk in his ways, we will experience his peace in our lives. In return, we will be less likely to give in to our own stubborn ways and desires, those things that cause us to stumble day in and day out. There is no reason to find ourselves stumbling head over heels as a result of our stubbornness. There is peace to be had! Why would we willingly choose not to partake of it?

Chapter 19

Lost and Found

What do you think? If a man has a hundred sheep, and one of them goes astray, does he not leave the ninety-nine and go to the mountains to seek the one that is straying? And if he should find it, assuredly, I say to you, he rejoices more over that sheep than over the ninety-nine that did not go astray.

—Matthew 18:12–13 (NKJV)

What a joy it has been to share my home with such a diverse menagerie of animals throughout the course of my life. To be blessed with the unconditional love of so many creatures is a rare treat, indeed. Every animal that has crossed my threshold has been loved completely, but also individually.

Sometimes when my children get together, they engage in a mock argument, trying to determine who my "favorite" is. As moms, we have no favorites, but I do offer a unique brand of love to each of our children, and in a way that is best received by each particular child. The same can be said for my pets.

While he was not necessarily my favorite, Casper was, by far, one of the dearest companions I've had the pleasure of loving. He had such a sweet disposition, hated the thought of disappointing his people, and had eyes that gave one the impression he possessed a very old soul.

He came to us as the proverbial stray dog, basically a bag of bones covered with too many fleas and ticks to count. He was skeptical of our intentions initially, but decided to take his chances and place his trust in us when we set up food, water, and a bed on the back porch for him. He could have left us that first night—there was nothing to prevent him from going. Our yard was not fenced at that time, and the screen doors on the porch were easy enough for him to escape through. But he chose to stick around and see what the future held for him here in the Simmons home.

Since it was apparent he was planning to stay a while, we took him to the vet to ensure he was up to date on vaccinations and to register him as the newest addition to our family.

Before giving him free rein of the house, we thought it would be best to give Casper a trial. We put his bed, a good sized bone, and a bowl of water in the master bathroom to see how he would respond to being in the house without us. In the morning before I left for work, he would walk into the bathroom with me, lie down on his bed, and follow me with his eyes as I walked out, closing the door behind me. When I returned home in the evening to let him out, he was usually lying on the bed, right where I left him. It was as if he didn't move from that spot at all during the day. After several weeks of proving his salt, it was time for the real test—leaving him in the house with the other dogs.

Like all animals—and humans, for that matter—he had his faults, and it was during this "real test" that we discovered his penchant for destruction. The first time we let him roam, we returned to find Ken's recliner half eaten. Casper was swiftly schooled on the inappropriateness of this behavior, and we purchased a new recliner. (Actually, we purchased twin recliners so I could have one, too. Mine would eventually become a safe haven for any dog needing to snuggle.)

And so, in our absence, Casper was relegated to the bathroom for a second time. When we felt he had learned the error of his ways, we gave him the opportunity to prove himself once more. This time we returned to find Ken's recliner half eaten—again. As you would expect, discipline and confinement followed.

He ate a little more of the recliner on at least one other occasion. That's when we decided it was time to pick our battles. He was perfectly content in the bathroom, and our house suffered no ill effects from this arrangement. It was a win-win situation, so we figured we should just go with it. Casper—1; Simmons'—0.

Another of his faults caused us to refer to him affectionately as Houdini. Shortly after his arrival on the scene, we put a fence around the backyard. Nothing fancy, just a barrier to keep our dogs in and other critters out. Ken tied the new fence into the pipe fence that surrounds the pasture, and the dogs ended up with a massive area to run and play in, safe and secure.

Day after day, I would come home from work to find three out of four dogs romping inside the fence while Casper sat in the front yard, excitedly wagging his tail at my arrival. And day after day, Ken would locate Casper's secret passage to freedom and come up with some creative way to seal it. Unfortunately, his efforts seemed always to be in vain because each day when I pulled into the driveway, that sweet-faced baby boy greeted me at my truck door, with his tail wagging so hard I thought he might actually take flight.

After much deliberation, we opted to give Casper the win on this one, too. He had obviously been on his own so long that he couldn't stand the thought of being fenced in. And since he never seemed to stray far from the house, we didn't really worry about it. That is, until the day he wandered a little too far off.

I came home from work one afternoon, surprised that a roly-poly white bundle of happiness was not waiting in the front yard to greet me with his tail wagging. I called for him, but he was apparently not within earshot because he didn't come running at the sound of my voice. After a half hour or so, I jumped back into the truck and started making the rounds. I searched the back roads, fields, and pastures around our property but found no leads on his whereabouts. With no other options available, I returned home to wait for him. After all, there was only one reason he would not return home, and I promptly pushed that idea completely out of my mind.

Nighttime fell heavy, and my heart fell right along with it. It was closing in on eleven o'clock, way past my bedtime, and was pitch black outside. I took one last stroll around the backyard, walking the fence line, peering into the pasture, and searching for some evidence that Casper was there in the darkness.

But there was no sign of him. Clearly, he was gone. Rather than allow myself to think the worst, I chose to believe he'd received from us the love and care he needed to get him back on his feet and moving on down the road. As I tried to make peace with this thought, turning to go back into the house, something caught my eye. In the pasture across the street, I could see the faint outline of a small, white animal making its way toward the house. I called out, "Casper!" and the dog quickened his step. In just a few seconds, he was at the front door, wagging that tail, wanting his mama. And his mama was just as eager to see him.

I can't put my finger on the reason this particular dog held such a cherished place in my heart, but he did. Something about him touched a place very deep inside me. He filled a need I hadn't even realized was there until he came along. During the time he was missing, when I didn't know if he was safe or not, that empty place inside me grew exponentially. I could not rest until he was back in my arms.

Isn't this just like the fierce love our Father has for us? We hold such a cherished place in the heart of God that when we stray from him, he won't rest until we have been brought back home where we belong. It may take years for us to come to our senses, repent of our sins, and come running into his outstretched arms. But when we do, he will rejoice over us with singing, and the angels will rejoice right along with him. Just as I watched and waited for my beloved Casper to return to the safety of our home, so our Father watches and waits for us to turn our hearts toward him.

Chapter 20

You Dirty Dog

Woe to you, teachers of the law and Pharisees, you hypocrites! You clean the outside of the cup and dish, but inside they are full of greed and self-indulgence.
—Matthew 23:25

Over the past couple of years, we have been saddened to see Sydney's sweet Baby Jayke become the victim of breed discrimination. His litter resulted from the breeding of an American Staffordshire terrier and an American bulldog. Our daughter was acquainted with the owners of these dogs, so we knew firsthand the peaceful, loving demeanor the parents would be passing along to their pups. We were very excited about bringing a new puppy into the family, though we were cautioned by well-meaning family members and friends about the dangers of owning a pit bull.

Maybe by now you have an idea of what our opinion is on this topic. We believe a dog of any breed can be a danger to others, just as sure as a dog of any breed can be a lifelong family companion. It's all in the training and the type of interaction that dog has with its people. Taking this to heart, we began Jayke's obedience training as soon as he entered our home, and he has been one of our most gifted students.

Oddly enough, we did not begin to refer to him as "Baby Jayke" when he was a puppy. It wasn't until he was older that the name was bestowed upon him. He possesses such a tender heart and has within him an insatiable desire to do the right thing. These are wonderful qualities for a companion animal to have, but they are also characteristics that can give the impression of timidity and weakness. As a result, Jayke was sometimes referred to as a baby in certain situations that included other, less compassionate dogs.

As a woman and nurturer, Sydney took the derogatory term and turned it into one of endearment. Hence, "Baby Jayke" was born.

We did not have a fenced yard when Baby Jayke came to us, so he and the other dogs would take turns tethered to a tie-down in the yard, enjoying the sunshine and fresh air for a short time each day. The area set aside for this happened to be on the same side of the house as one of the freestanding water spigots.

This would be a good time to tell you that Jayke loves water. I mean Jayke *really* loves water. If you think you are going to water the outdoor plants with the hose while Jayke is outside with you, you've got another think coming. It ain't gonna happen. He will try to eat the water as it comes out of the hose. And if he can't make that work for him, he'll just eat the hose instead. Sometimes to entertain ourselves, we hold the hose up to create a stream of water that sprays straight into the air. Jayke catches sight of it and runs toward the water at top speed. Then, jumping higher than gravity should allow, he leaps into the stream, writhing around in midair, chomping at the water like an angry crocodile. He just loves water.

Jayke had reached his turn in the rotation for fresh air and sunshine one afternoon, so Sydney took him out and attached his collar to the lead, and he began to roll around in the grass, enjoying his dogness. He stayed out for about half an hour or so while we did some housekeeping, then I went out to retrieve him.

Apparently, the spigot had developed a slow leak that had gone unnoticed by everyone in our house—except Baby Jayke. Boy, was I surprised when I rounded the corner to find not a white dog with brindle markings but a dark brown dog with only a touch of white on the very top of his head. He had noticed the leaky faucet, which had created a nice little mud hole under it, and had proceeded to roll in it, lay in it, dig in it, chomp at it. You get the idea. I was met by our sweet Baby Jayke, sitting patiently at the end of the lead for me to release him to come back into the house.

I couldn't help it. Right there in the middle of the yard, I threw back my head and roared with laughter. Then, I immediately reached in my back pocket and grabbed my phone for the best photo op of the summer.

Underneath all that filth and mud, the purest heart that could ever be found in an animal was steadily beating. Baby Jayke may have looked like a dirty dog, but that was no reflection of what existed deep within him. We knew, on his inside, he was filled with innocence and goodness— he was clean, wholesome, untainted. But he sure didn't look that way on the outside.

Just like Baby Jayke, we sometimes give an outward appearance that isn't an accurate representation of the person we are on the inside. Regrettably, our theatrical production is frequently seen in reverse. We put on our Sunday best and plaster on our most charming smile as we "act justly and love mercy and walk humbly with our God" (Mic. 6:8). In doing this, we give others the impression that we have it all together, that we are on the fast-track to heaven. But if they could see past the exterior and into our hearts, where we occasionally harbor jealousy, envy, and greed, and where we hide our real motivation of selfish ambition, they would see the truth: we offer a great deal of curb appeal, but we haven't even pulled out the cleaning supplies needed to tackle the inside of the house.

Jesus reminds us that it's not enough to look polished on the outside while harboring hatred and selfishness in our hearts. We are called to reflect the beauty of Christ from the inside out, and to do so, we must start with the heart. Our hearts give the true reflection of who we are as people. Proverbs 27:19 tells us, "As water reflects the face, so one's life reflects the heart." We can certainly have a pleasing appearance, but how much sweeter it will be when our hearts, minds, and souls are just as pleasing!

Let the record show that Baby Jayke got a good scrubbing before he was brought back into the house that afternoon. When it was all said and done, the beauty of his heart matched the beauty of his shiny, white coat perfectly—just as it should.

Chapter 21

Thank You

In everything give thanks; for this is the will of God in Christ Jesus for you.
——I Thessalonians 5:18 (NKJV)

One of the things Dixie and I share in common is our love of fine cuisine. Actually, it doesn't even have to be fine. It can be mediocre. We enjoy just about anything that can be considered edible. For the most part, we go to bed with full bellies, completely satisfied, thinking we won't need another meal for at least two days. Then the alarm goes off, and we wake up famished! We can't seem to get to the kitchen fast enough. Just a word of caution. If you're ever at our house first thing in the morning, make sure you're not blocking the path between us and the refrigerator!

When Dixie first came to us, she was a scrawny little pup. Our first objective was to put some weight on her. And that's exactly what we did. That baby girl ate to her heart's content—and her tummy's too! We far surpassed our goal of fattening her up a bit. As a matter of fact, a few months ago, our vet told us we needed to put her on a diet. In his opinion, she was just too young to be struggling with weight issues, which could potentially lead to more serious issues down the road. He suggested we cut back her food consumption just until we could see her waist again. So we followed the good doctor's orders and moved her from three meals a day to only two. And in the words of my wise and witty father, that went over like a lead balloon.

But in those early days, before we had to limit her calorie intake and she was allowed to eat until her little tummy got full, she did this weird thing after her morning meal. We're honestly not sure if it's a Weimaraner thing or just a Dixie thing, but it was definitely a "get your attention and make you chuckle" thing.

Dixie would wake us up for breakfast by putting her front paws on the bed and nuzzling us with her nose. Ken and I would take turns feeding her in the wee hours of the morning, so whomever was responsible for her grub that day would get up, fill her bowl, then return to the warmth of the bed.

We could hear Dixie scarfing down her food, making sure she didn't miss a single kibble. The sound was similar to that of a vacuum cleaner being run at top speed over a stainless steel surface. Once she had sufficiently cleaned her bowl, we would experience a brief moment of silence, followed by a long, low, soulful howl. If you listened carefully, you could almost hear the gratitude she was trying to convey.

This is how the cycle worked: she would wake up starving every morning; we would provide her with sustenance; and she would be genuinely grateful that we had met her physical need. She always made a point of giving thanks for her provision.

How often do I forget to give thanks to my Father for the provisions I receive from him on a daily basis? It seems the everyday things are often taken for granted. Instead of being considered thoughtful gifts from God, which they truly are, they are viewed as stuff that has been made available to us to help us survive and nothing more.

A few months ago, I was challenged by a Facebook friend to take the "Attitude of Gratitude" challenge. This task requires you to list three things you are grateful for each day, for five consecutive days. It was a real eye-opener for me. Although I stopped posting my list on my Facebook page after the fifth day, I did not let my attitude of gratitude come to a screeching halt. I continued to count my blessings.

As a result, I have been amazed at the multitude of blessings God drops in my lap each and every day. Some of them are big, like the recent employment opportunity that came along at just the right time. Some are seemingly small, like finding a pocketknife in the laundry hamper that had been MIA for days. The size of the blessing is not what's important. The fact that we recognize it as a personal gift directly from the hand of God is what's important.

In *everything* give thanks: in the big, the small, the silly, the spectacular, the miraculous—in everything. Do you feel like you have nothing to be thankful for? If so, take just a moment to glance around you right where you are.

Are you sitting in a house that is warm in the winter and cool in the summer? Do you have a bed to sleep in at night, with at least one pillow and blanket? Does your refrigerator and/or pantry have food in it? Is there a vehicle in your driveway that gets you from point A to point B as needed? Are you capable of reading the book you hold in your hands right now? Could you get out of bed, get dressed, and make yourself presentable to the public without the aid of another person? Did you wake up this morning, once more drawing the breath of life into your lungs? If you answered yes to any of these, my friend, you have been showered with blessings from the Almighty.

Don't forget to thank him when you recognize these gifts. Go ahead, throw your head back, and give God a long, low, soulful thank you. While you're at it, plan to take your own Attitude of Gratitude challenge. Just don't limit yourself to three things each day. Take a good, hard look around you, and you'll be surprised at how many blessings you'll be able to count.

Chapter 22

I'm Thirstin' to Death

*As the deer pants for streams of water, so my soul
pants for you, my God. My soul thirsts for God, for
the living God. When can I go and meet with God?*
—Psalm 42:1–2

There is nothing in the world like a cool drink of water after a long, hard day working in the heat. If you've ever had the task of raking up grass clippings or pulling weeds from the flower beds under a midday Texas sun, you know just how refreshing a simple glass of water can be.

Growing up, my sisters and I often exaggerated our physical state when pleading with our parents for something we wanted. "Mom, when is dinner? I'm starving to death!"

And of course, if you could starve to death, certainly you could also thirst to death. "Dad, can we stop at McDonalds for a Coke? I'm thirstin' to death!"

I think of this phrase every time I let the dogs back into the house after spending the day outdoors. We always ensure that they have an adequate supply of water while they are outside, but it doesn't ever seem to be enough. Once they are inside, in the comfort of a cool house, they make a mad dash to the water bowls and start lapping up the refreshing liquid held within.

The dogs have individual, personalized food and water dishes, and that's where each begins to cool down. But after a few drinks from his or her own bowl, each quickly takes a turn at all the others in rotation. Leaving a trail of water behind, they dash from one dish to the next, as if they will never be able to quench their thirst.

Watching them move from station to station the way they do, you would think each bowl offered a different flavor or something. Even though they have all been filled from the same faucet, the dogs run from one to another as if they were being presented with a unique taste experience at each stop. If I hadn't filled them myself, I'd think they were making their rounds at a soda fountain—from lemonade to iced tea to cherry limeade!

Once they have finally satisfied their need for refreshment, they crash on the tile floor in an effort to cool off. As they lie there, the sound of panting can easily be heard throughout the house. The dogs use fluid intake to attain an immediate reduction in body temperature, but because they cannot sweat, they must pant to continue the cool down process.

To pant is to breathe hard and quick, especially after physical exertion of some sort. This is the type of panting the dogs experience after running around outside all day. However, an alternate definition of panting, according to dictionary.reference.com, is "to long with breathless or intense eagerness; yearn."

Psalm 42:1 begins, "As the deer pants for streams of water, so my soul pants for you, my God." This refers to a deer with a yearning, a deep desire, to find a source of refreshment. We should yearn for fellowship with God with this same breathless eagerness.

Dixie, Bexar, and Ty rush into the house in search of fresh water with the same urgency we should have as we seek out God's companionship. We should be filled with excitement at the prospect of meeting with him, because every time we do, we are each offered a unique taste of his goodness—his love, his mercy, his hope, his grace—even though it is coming from only one source.

What if our relationship with God was such that we experienced an ache inside, a true yearning, to be with him? What if we couldn't wait for the next time we would get to share a moment with him? I don't know about you, but I want my desire for communion with my Father to become an unquenchable thirst. I want to long for it with breathless and intense eagerness, just as the dogs pant for bowls of cool water after a long day in the heat of a summer sun. I want to be refreshed, not by what the world has to offer, but by what God alone can give.

Chapter 23

The Lord Gave and the Lord Has Taken Away

The Lord gave and the Lord has taken away; may the name of the Lord be praised.
—Job 1:21

There are so many things that come and go during the course of our lives. Immediately, my thoughts fall on those I have deeply loved and lost over the years—my wonderful father, all four of my grandparents, two dear aunts, and a myriad of others. Then there are the many close friends I've lost touch with along the way, either because of relocation or, to be honest, just plain neglect.

Aside from people, there are literal "things" that have passed through my life for a limited time. Homes, vehicles, pieces of furniture, articles of clothing—all of these items helped to define me in one way or another. That papasan chair announced to anyone who walked into my living room, "She's all about comfort." The gold nugget ring in the shape of Texas let all who saw it know I was (and still am) completely devoted to my home state. And let's not forget the Darth Vader voice-changing helmet that ensured my obsession with Star Wars didn't go unnoticed.

We acquire so much living these lives of ours, and as we do, often times we truly believe we will hold on to those things forever. So cherished are they that we can't possibly imagine our lives without them. But occasionally, we find ourselves in a position that requires us to let go of some of those precious possessions. Only by the grace of God do we somehow manage to survive without them. Many times, he even brings something new into our lives, not as a replacement necessarily, but perhaps as an exchange of sorts.

As I look back on all the animals I've had the privilege of caring for, I see the way each one affected the particular season of my life he entered into. I also see how God healed my heart after the loss of each one.

When I was very young, we acquired our first dog. He was a fox terrier mix, fawn colored with a white chest and white-tipped tail. We named him Grover. We were told in no uncertain terms by our mother that Grover was to be an outdoor dog. He was not to enter the house at any time for any reason. "Yes, ma'am." (Wink, wink!) All it took was one cold, winter night to melt her heart and toss that rule right out the window. Grover spent his entire life with us. We were the only family he ever knew. In my youth, he gave me something to care for and helped me learn responsibility. And as my first dog, I give him credit for making me such an enthusiastic lover of canines decades later.

Samson was another fine animal I feel honored to have housed. He was a full-blooded Boxer that we purchased, along with his sister, when the girls were very young. What a fantastic babysitter he was. He had the sweetest spirit I've ever seen in a large dog. My father was especially fond of Samson, though I really do not have the slightest idea why. I can tell you that Samson returned his adoration. (But then again, my dad has always been pretty irresistible.) As Samson got up in years, he began to have health issues, including seizures and congestive heart failure. Rather than have him suffer through the unpredictable attacks and possibly cause injury to himself, we made the decision to have him put down. I remember walking into the vet's office, with Sydney and Samson by my side, and completely breaking down when the receptionist asked if she could help us. She quickly grabbed a box of Kleenex, ushered us into a room, and told us to take all the time we needed to tell Samson goodbye. We knew we were making the right decision, but it was heartbreaking, just the same. Samson was a silent yet steady companion during a very difficult time for our family.

Shortly after losing Samson, I met my sweet husband, Ken, and was introduced to Calamity Jane. All it took was a couple of McDonald's cheeseburgers for us to become fast friends. Devoted companion that she was, she didn't like to be too far from Ken, which meant she also spent a good bit of her time close to me as well. In her own special way, Calamity helped me pick up the pieces of my life and start all over again. She lived a long and contented life before cancer took her from us, and once more, I endured a teary-eyed farewell to a faithful friend.

Fortunately for our tender hearts, we had introduced Mocha into the family a couple of years before losing Calamity. Different from all the dogs Ken and I have collectively owned throughout our lives, Mocha struck a chord with both of us and managed to steal our hearts in a very unique way. She seemed to be shrouded with a veil of innocence that could not be explained. She also spent the remainder of her days with our family, leaving us only after we determined she was experiencing kidney failure. In the time I spent with her, Mocha taught me important lessons about acceptance.

So many joyful hellos; so many tearful goodbyes. Job knew firsthand what he was talking about when he said "the Lord gave and the Lord has taken away." We will never know what God's ultimate plans are for us—only that he has plans to prosper us and not to harm us (Jer. 29:11). In our confusion, it becomes very easy to question, "Why, Lord, would you take this beautiful creature from me? Why give her to me at all, allowing me to experience the fullness of her affection for only a short time, if you were just going to strip her from me in the end?"

Many times we use Job's words to help assuage our grief, to explain loss. But we fail to look at the phrase that immediately follows this statement of give and take: "May the name of the Lord be praised." Job had lost everything—his wealth, his home, his livestock, his storehouses, his family—yet he continued to give praise to God. We are told that through everything that happened to him, Job did not sin or blame God (1:22).

Job must have recognized that God's purposes are bigger than anything we could ever imagine, and that we must trust in his goodness, regardless of what we are going through. No matter how bleak our circumstances seem to be, we can only see the here and now. God sees all the way to the end. He knows how things will play out. Because we know this, we can look adversity in the face and say, "May the name of the Lord be praised."

Chapter 24

Your People Will
Be My People

But Ruth replied, "Don't urge me to leave you or to turn back from you. Where you go I will go, and where you stay I will stay. Your people will be my people and your God my God."

—Ruth 1:16

Moving away from home is one of the most difficult choices we make in life. We willingly decide to leave the only life we've ever known and venture into the great unknown. We step out of our comfort zone to embark on a journey that is completely new to us. It is exciting and mysterious and frightening and nerve-racking, all at the same time.

I can't help but wonder what it must be like for an animal to be asked to leave his home and relocate to a new place, with new people, and perhaps even new animals. If we experience such a wide range of emotions when we knowingly move to a new environment, it only makes sense that such an abrupt disruption in a pet's life would have the potential to be traumatic.

In my mind, I imagine dogs that have been rescued from shelters have an easier time adjusting to a new home. They have been cared for by several different people while in the shelter and have seen strangers come and go as they "shop" for the perfect family pet. Being with new people probably wouldn't be too scary for those animals. It's the ones who have settled into a routine with a family that I believe could potentially have a difficult time adjusting to a new life. This is how I believe it was for Mocha.

Mocha belonged to a coworker of ours. Though I don't remember the details of her history prior to being in our friend's home, I do recall him mentioning an atmosphere of domestic violence in her past. This was evident by her fear of going through doors that were not fully open, as if she had been harshly pushed through a threshold and injured by the door in the process. She was also extremely head shy. It took us a couple of years to break her of ducking when we attempted to pet her on top of the head. And her overall demeanor was one that suggested she just wanted to get through the day without making anyone mad.

She was given to us for a couple of reasons. First of all, we were told she was a digger and was wreaking havoc on our friend's yard. Second, his daughter was in the market for a puppy, and Mocha was an "old lady." Given that information, what choice did we have but to take her in?

And so it was that Mocha became a Simmons. It wasn't because she was seeking out a change of pace. Circumstances beyond her control forced her to shift into a completely new atmosphere. She didn't know anything about our home, how we operated, or what kind of "parents" we would be.

Am I the only one who wonders whether or not she was nervous or scared when she walked through our door? Regardless of any internal struggle she may have been going through during the transition, she showed up wearing her most irresistible Mocha face and won us over on the spot. We experienced a two-way adoption process. We didn't just claim Mocha as our own, she also accepted us as her trustworthy providers, her brand new family.

Much like Ruth, Mocha was at a crossroads in her canine life that required a life-altering decision to be made. Of course, Mocha's owner made the decision on her behalf, but she still had to deal with the initial adjustment to life in the country. And at some point, she had to make up her mind to go where we went and stay where we stayed.

It didn't take too long for her to do just that. As a matter of fact, she even attended Valley View High School with Sydney one day. She rode the bus and everything. She was part of a drama assignment that required Sydney to make a presentation about the three most important things in her life. Mocha happened to be number one.

When we reach a crossroads in life, it is important to surround ourselves with godly people so we can follow in their footsteps, paying close attention to the ways they stay focused on his will. We want to learn to go where they go, stay where they stay, let their God be our God and let their people be our people.

It is easy to become frightened or anxious when faced with the unknown, but if we have learned to rely on the fellowship of other believers, we can face uncertainty with confidence. We have a support system at the ready to approach the throne of God on our behalf. They will lift up our concerns and insecurities and ask that they be replaced with confidence and assurance. Then, before you know it, you will be able to put on your most irresistible face and walk right through the door of the unknown, ready to meet your new adventure.

Chapter 25

Fill Me with Compassion

But a Samaritan, as he traveled, came where the man was; and when he saw him, he took pity on him. He went to him and bandaged his wounds, pouring on oil and wine. Then he put the man on his own donkey, brought him to an inn and took care of him.
—Luke 10:33–34

I've noticed that as I get older, I tend to be less and less tolerant of pettiness, negativity, and drama in general. Maybe it's the realization of my own mortality, knowing I'm no longer a spring chicken and that my days are numbered. I don't want to waste a single minute on things that don't add value to my life.

Maybe it's all the wisdom that I've acquired over the years, telling me that there are some things that just shouldn't be tolerated. Period. Some things should be called out, brought into the light, and seen as the dangers they truly are.

On the flip side, there are things I definitely need to abide. This list includes people who sometimes rub me the wrong way. We all have those people in our lives, and though we try our dead level best to enjoy their company, it's more difficult some days than others. God calls us to love one another, just as Christ loved us. It's simple, but it's not always easy.

Thankfully, God instilled in us a little something to kick-start our hearts and get us moving in the right direction. It's called compassion. Webster's dictionary tells us that compassion is "a feeling of wanting to help someone who is sick, hungry, in trouble, etc." As odd as it sounds, seeing someone endure hardship sometimes makes it easier for us to reach out to them and offer a helping hand. That's what we witnessed between Calamity Jane and Bexar.

Bexar originally belonged to our daughter Kimberly. He was her pick of a litter of pups being given away in front of our local Walmart. She scanned the group until her eyes rested on the biggest, fattest, fuzziest one in the bunch. He looked like a miniature black bear cub. Turns out his size wasn't the only thing that was large about this guy. We soon discovered he was a huge whiner, as well.

Kimberly tried her best to crate train him, but soon gave in to his whimpering and put the kennel away. At least by allowing him to join her at night, they were both able to get a good night's sleep.

The two of them became almost inseparable. Bexar hated to watch Kimberly leave for school in the mornings and got so excited when he saw me grab my keys in the afternoon so we could go pick her up. As soon as he saw her emerge from the building, that little tail would start wagging so hard you would think his entire rear end was going to break off at any minute.

Once she was in the car, he couldn't get quite close enough to her. He always seemed to end up curled around her neck, his head draped over one shoulder and his tail over the other. Instead of mink, it looked like she was wearing a mutt stole.

All of this took place during the latter part of Kimberly's senior year of high school. As we neared graduation day, plans were made for both of the girls to return to Georgia with their Nana the day after the commencement exercises for a long-term visit, sans puppy. Bright and early that Saturday morning and with a heavy heart, Kimberly gave her goodbye kisses, waved farewell to Bexar, and headed east.

It didn't take long for us to notice a change in Bexar that morning. He seemed to have very little energy, spending most of his day just lying around. Calamity Jane also noticed this and responded with more concern than we did. We assumed he was feeling lost without Kimberly, like he sometimes did while she was at school during the day. But Calamity's keen senses were telling her something different, so she stayed very close by him.

A few hours after we noticed the lethargy, little Bexar began to pass very loose stools and to lose his stomach contents, which consisted mostly of bile since he hadn't eaten since the night before. We tried to keep him hydrated, but he was unable to keep even water down.

At this point, we did the worst possible thing anyone can do in a situation like this. We consulted Google. Of course, within minutes we were sure we were dealing with parvovirus or distemper and that Bexar wouldn't make it through the night. We took his temperature, and it confirmed what Google had already told us the temperature of a dying pup would be. It was time to call Kimberly to let her know what the situation was with Bexar and to discuss options for how to handle treatment. As we talked with her, Calamity paced nervously beside the ailing puppy, never taking her eyes off him.

It was determined we would take him to the animal emergency clinic in Denton, so Ken gathered up this lifeless form, wrapped him in a blanket, and placed him in my lap for the trip to the city. When we arrived, we were given their proposed plan of action and the cost associated with it. We explained to them that this baby's mom was only eighteen-years-old and on a budget—a very tight one at that. The staff was gracious enough to do everything they felt was necessary for whatever Kimberly was able to fit into her budget. We were told they would administer intravenous fluids along with the appropriate medications and call us with an update on his state later that night, then again first thing in the morning. Reluctantly, we left Bexar in their capable hands and made the drive back home. The late night update was neither positive nor negative. They told us his IV was running and he was comfortable, but there was no noticeable change in his condition.

Morning came, and we awoke feeling apprehensive. If Bexar survived the night, it would be nothing short of a miracle. The telephone rang, and we braced ourselves for the bad news, trying to work out in our heads how we would tell Kimberly she had lost her puppy. Instead, we heard the technician say Bexar was making slight improvement and they would like to keep him until four o'clock that afternoon, to ensure his recovery continued moving in the right direction. We made the necessary arrangements and then breathed a sigh of relief. Calamity, on the other hand, had no way of knowing Bexar was going to be all right. She continued to pace the floor, and the worry she felt for that pup was evident in her behavior.

It must be said at this time that there was no love lost between Calamity Jane and Bexar. She was the grouchy old dog, and he was the spunky, new puppy. And if there were two words Calamity detested, they were "spunky" and "puppy." She would growl at Bexar any time he started to approach her. And Bexar wouldn't even come into a room if Calamity was near the door, for fear of being snapped at. They were different. If they were cast for parts in a play about the good Samaritan, Bexar would have been the man who was beaten up, and Calamity would have been the priest or the Levite. She felt such bitterness toward Bexar for invading and disrupting her home that she wouldn't have shed a tear for Bexar in his suffering, just as the priest and Levite saw the beaten man and passed him by, even going so far as to cross the road to be farther from him when they passed.

Except this time, Calamity proved not to be the priest or the Levite. She proved to be the Samaritan, the Good Samaritan.

When we walked out of the house Sunday afternoon to pick Bexar up at the animal hospital, we left Calamity Jane behind, still in a state of anxiety. About two hours later, we returned with a very tired but convalescing puppy. We got him into the house and laid him down on one of the dog beds. Before his four paws hit the pillow, his arch nemesis was at his side, smelling and licking and satisfying her need to know he was really home and that he was going to be okay after all. She stayed there the rest of the evening and made a point of checking on him intermittently, throughout the night.

It was only because of Bexar's suffering that Calamity was able to set aside her negative feelings for this new family member, seeing him as one of God's precious creations, deserving of the love and respect of others. What a lesson there is to be learned there. But why wait until misfortune befalls those we have issues with to demonstrate the love and mercy of our heavenly Father? Why not show them, in every circumstance, the unconditional love of Christ that he showered on us from the cross?

Afterword

It is my hope that you found this collection of stories enjoyable and that they brought a smile to your face. For those of you who daily share my walk with God, I also hope you found encouragement in the scriptures that were selected to bring spiritual relevance to the seemingly ordinary, day-to-day experiences life presents us with.

Or perhaps you have finished this book and now realize you do not have a relationship with God. Maybe as you look back on your life, you cannot remember a time when you determined to give your heart and soul to Jesus Christ, accepting him as your personal Savior. Dear friend, if you are lost in this world and are seeking salvation from the only one who can give it, then I would like to leave you with the resources you need to become a Christian.

As a young child, I learned the ABCs of becoming a follower of Christ. The steps are simple and easy enough for a child to understand.

A. Admit that you are a sinner.
B. Believe that Christ died to save you.
C. Confess to others that you are a Christian.

Sounds simple enough, right? Maybe a little too simple: ABC and I'm going to heaven when I die.

So all can fully understand the significance of this decision, let me give you the biblical foundation behind the process. You can find all the information you need in the book of Romans, so pick up a New Testament, and let's take a stroll down the "Romans Road to Salvation."

When we reach the end of this road, you'll have a deeper understanding of why we need salvation, how it became available to us, what we must do in order to receive it and how our daily lives will be affected by it.

1. **Romans 3:23: "For all have sinned and fall short of the glory of God."** First things first. We must admit we are sinners. We have all disobeyed and displeased God. Sure, we're good people deep down. We give to the Salvation Army at Christmastime; we help people we see on the side of the road with their car hood up; we even take

in abandoned animals in need of loving homes. That's all well and good, but it doesn't change the facts: we are all sinners. Some of us have a hard time with this first step of admission. How about picking up that New Testament real quick and reading through Romans 3:10–18 to see if you really do fit into the category of "sinner" with the rest of us. You may be surprised.

2. **Romans 6:23: "For the wages of sin is death, but the gift of God is eternal life in Jesus Christ our Lord."** Every wrong deed has a punishment attached to it. We learned this truth the first time we snuck a cookie after our mom told us not to. Our sin also has a punishment attached to it: death. Apart from Christ, our physical death results in eternal separation from God, sentenced to spend eternity in hell.

3. **Romans 5:8: "But God demonstrates His own love for us in this: While we were still sinners, Christ died for us."** Hang on, there is good news. Rather than having us pay the penalty for our own sin, Christ himself bore the responsibility so we wouldn't have to. He sacrificially gave up his life so we would not have to endure eternal damnation as the result of our sin.

4. **Romans 10:9: "If you declare with your mouth, 'Jesus is Lord,' and believe in your heart that**

God raised him from the dead, you will be saved." Romans 10:13: "For everyone who calls on the name of the Lord will be saved." My dad liked to say "just believe and receive." It really is that simple. When Jesus died on the cross, he paid the penalty for our sins. Through his death, we were spared an eternity in hell and were given the gift of salvation. This gift is available to anyone who wants it. There are no exclusions. All we have to do is believe and receive.

5. **Romans 5:1: "Therefore, since we have been justified through faith, we have peace with God through our Lord Jesus Christ."** After receiving the gift of salvation, you will begin to experience a peace unlike any other, which only comes from a relationship with Jesus Christ. But there is something even greater that salvation brings. Freedom from condemnation. **Romans 8:1** tells us, **"Therefore, there is now no condemnation for those who are in Christ Jesus."** If you are familiar with the concept of double jeopardy (not the game show), this will make sense to you. Once someone has paid the penalty for a crime, he or she cannot be brought to trial for that crime again. There can be no further condemnation for that person because the penalty has been satisfied, either by acquittal or conviction. Since Jesus paid

the price for our sins—past, present, and future—as followers of Christ, we cannot be asked to stand trial for those sins. The penalty imposed by them has been satisfied by Christ, once and for all.

6. **Finally, Romans 8:38–39: "For I am convinced that neither death nor life, neither angels nor demons, neither the present nor the future, nor any powers, neither height nor depth, nor anything else in all creation, will be able to separate us from the love of God that is in Christ Jesus our Lord."** As is often the case, the Romans Road saves the very best news for last. As you begin to delve into God's word, you will find it is riddled with promises he wants his children to claim. This is by far one of the best. Once we receive the salvation Christ made available to us, there is nothing that can ever separate us from God's everlasting love. Nothing at all. As believers in Christ, the love of God dwells in us; it becomes a part of our very makeup and begins to define who we are as Christians.

We have reached the end of the Romans Road to Salvation. That's all there is to it. See, simple enough for a child to understand. Now that you have the directions, you can follow them to a new life in Christ. Not sure how to do that? There is a very simple prayer you can pray directly to God, wherever you are. You don't have to have a degree in theology or brush up on your thees and thous. Just talk to God like you would an old friend. After all, he's known you for your entire life, whether you ever acknowledged him before today or not. You just need to remember the ABCs: Acknowledge that you're a sinner—tell God you know you've done wrong in his eyes. Believe Christ died for your sin—let him know you believe in the sacrifice Christ made that allowed you this opportunity for salvation today. Confess to others that you are a Christian—promise to share your good news with others. Remember, without belief this prayer is merely a smattering of words on a page. Salvation comes only through believing. If you have followed the Romans Road straight to the foot of the cross and want to accept Christ into your heart, you can pray this prayer:

> Dear Lord, I realize that I am a sinner. I have done things that are wrong in your eyes. I know that the punishment for sin is death. I believe that you sent your only son, Jesus, to die on the cross for me, so I would not have to pay the price for my sin, but have eternal life by simply believing in you. I ask you to forgive me of my sin and come into my heart. I want to accept your gift of salvation. Please help me to follow your ways and to live the kind of life you want me to live. Thank

you for loving me enough to make a way for me to become a child of yours. I can't wait to spend eternity with you. Amen.

Acknowledgments

I would like to take a moment to thank some very special people whose encouragement led to the writing of this book. Without their help and support, the book in your hands would never have gone to print.

- My father, Richard Call, who did not live to see this dream become a reality, but maintained a very clear vision of its completion in his mind
- My mother, Cherrie Call, who started believing in me at birth and has yet to stop
- My husband, Ken Simmons, who continually puts my dreams and desires above his own and wishes only to see me fly

- My sisters, Charolette Kirby, Celeste Wilson, and Amy Womack, who are always there to pick me up when I fall down (after laughing hysterically, of course) and set me back on the right track

- My aunt, Beverly Wofford, who has always found ways to spark and support my creativity

- My aunt, Billie Balme, who has come to my grammatical rescue on numerous occasions

- All of my children, who bring untold joy to my life, filling my days with the fondest of memories and gut-busting laughter: Brady, Sydney, Kimberly, Nick, Brooke and Kenny

- Bryan Dodge, who had no idea he would hold the key to bringing this book to life, and lastly

- Those beloved animals who have brought more blessings to this woman's life than I could possibly deserve.

Special Thanks

Heartfelt thanks also goes out to the following people and/ or groups who helped bring this book to life by offering technical, editorial, and/or financial support:

Amy Womack
Beverly Wofford
Bill & Bobbie Wofford
Billie Balme
Brady Sharp
Brenda Fowler
Brooke Simmons
Carol Womack
Charolette Kirby
Cherrie Call

Cheryl Spruiell

Darrell Ryan

Freida Jensen

Ken Simmons

Kristi Wood

Lee Ann Dempsey

Lisa Elzroth

Lynn Schwab

Mary Martinez

Skip & Mardie Ussery

Wanda Mertes

The Slidely Team (slidely.com)

The Women's Bible Study group at Riding for the Brand Cowboy Church